Best O' Brown
to you.
Bill Thomas

The Brown County Book

by Bill Thomas

Indiana University Press   Bloomington

Copyright © 1981 by Bill Thomas
All rights reserved
No part of this book may be reproduced or utilized in any form or by any means, electronic or mechanical, including photocopying and recording, or by any information storage and retrieval system, without permission in writing from the publisher. The Association of American University Presses' Resolution on Permissions constitutes the only exception to this prohibition.
Manufactured in the United States of America

Library of Congress Cataloging in Publication Data
Thomas, Bill, 1934-
　　The Brown County book.
　　1. Brown County (Ind.)　　I. Title.
F532.B76T47　　　　977.2'253　　　　81-47292
ISBN 0-253-10546-3　　　　　　　　AACR2
ISBN 0-253-20269-8 (pbk.)
1　2　3　4　5　85　84　83　82　81

ACKNOWLEDGMENTS

A book is seldom the creation of the author alone. Many thoughts from many minds bring about its reality. It was no different for The Brown County Book. *The author hereby wishes to extend his heartfelt thanks to those who so kindly contributed their time and effort to this work. They include:*

Jack McDonald of Bean Blossom, Judge Sam Rosen, Mira Stefaniuk, Brenda Braughton of Indianapolis, James Stamper, Barbara Sheehan, Mary Richhart, Herman Dine, Sandy Brown, George Stephens, Edna Frazier, Bobbie Taylor, Marilyn Braun, Stu Huffman, Greg Temple, Karen Norman, Louise and George Kissling, Emma Moore, Pat Richardson, James Richardson, Tom Hubbard, Bill Henderson, Norma Gardner, Sue Shelden, Phil Desch, Howard Poole, Lee Nading, The Folklore Institute, Mike Ellis, Jim Eagelman, Dorothy Bailey, Don Stoffer, Jack Brubaker, John Mills, jack Weddle, Rex Kritzer, Wilbur Followell, Frank Chitwood, Helen Ayers, Don Goodwin, Ralph Yoder, Mrs. Jack Cullum and James (Junior) Cullum, Trish Barr, Mike Nickels, Jess Allen, William Lee, and Roger Shipley.

My special thanks to my wife, Phyllis, and my son Alan for their assistance on this project.

To Those Precious Few

Who Would Preserve Some of the Antiquity

And Atmosphere That is Brown County

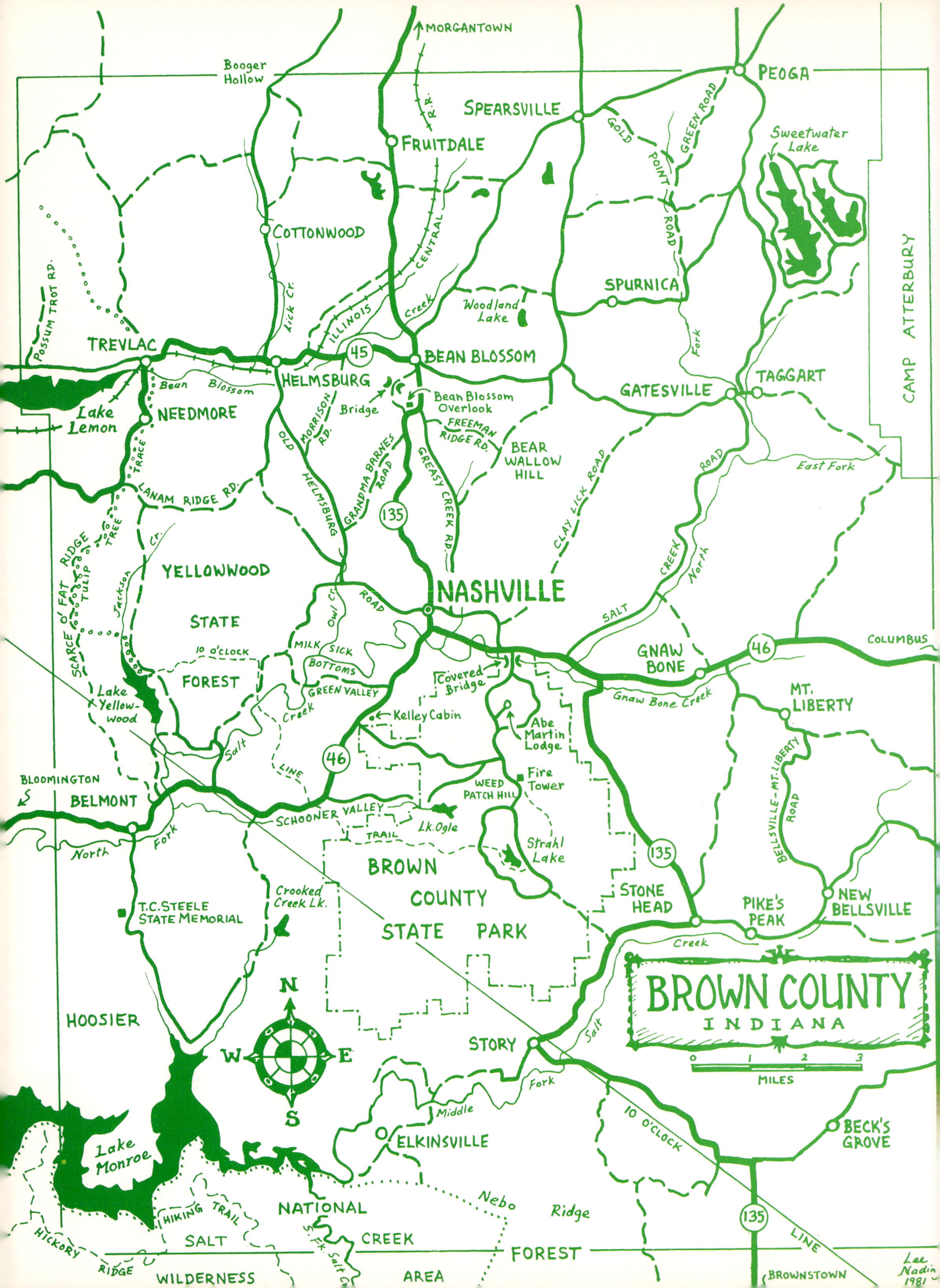

MORGANTOWN
Booger Hollow
PEOGA
SPEARSVILLE
FRUITDALE
R.R.
GOLD POINT ROAD
GREEN ROAD
Sweetwater Lake
COTTONWOOD
ILLINOIS CENTRAL
Lick Cr.
Creek
SPURNICA
Woodland Lake
CAMP ATTERBURY
POSSUM TROT RD.
TREVLAC
45
HELMSBURG
BEAN BLOSSOM
Fork
TAGGART
GATESVILLE
Bean Blossom
Lake Lemon
NEEDMORE
Bridge
Bean Blossom Overlook
MORRISON RD.
OLD HELMSBURG
GRANDMA BARNES ROAD
GREASY CREEK RD.
FREEMAN RIDGE RD.
BEAR WALLOW HILL
TRACE
LANAM RIDGE RD.
CLAY LICK ROAD
ROAD
East Fork
135
TULIP TREE
SCARCE O' FAT RIDGE
Jackson
Cr.
YELLOWWOOD STATE FOREST
NASHVILLE
Owl Cr.
ROAD
SALT CREEK
North
10 O'CLOCK
MILK SICK BOTTOMS
GREEN VALLEY
Covered Bridge
GNAW BONE
46
COLUMBUS
Gnaw Bone Creek
MT. LIBERTY
Lake Yellowwood
Kelley Cabin
Creek
Salt
Abe Martin Lodge
LINE
BLOOMINGTON
BELMONT
Fire Tower
WEED PATCH HILL
SCHOONER VALLEY TRAIL
Lk. Ogle
BELLSVILLE-MT. LIBERTY ROAD
North Fork
Strahl Lake
BROWN COUNTY STATE PARK
STONE HEAD
PIKE'S PEAK
NEW BELLSVILLE
Crooked Creek Lk.
T.C. STEELE STATE MEMORIAL
Creek
BROWN COUNTY
INDIANA
0 1 2 3
MILES
HOOSIER
N
W
E
S
STORY
Salt
Fork
Middle
10 O'CLOCK LINE
BECK'S GROVE
ELKINSVILLE
Lake Monroe
NATIONAL
Nebo Ridge
HIKING TRAIL
SALT CREEK
HICKORY RIDGE
FOREST
WILDERNESS
AREA
S. Fk. Salt Cr.
BROWNSTOWN
Lee Nading 1981

Contents

1. Brown County—The Place — *18*
2. The Three Giants — *39*
3. The Wooded Playground — *49*
4. Those Other Artists — *57*
5. People & Lifestyles — *65*
6. Folklore, Legends, & Other Stuff — *75*
7. Potpourri — *85*
8. Food & Recipes — *91*

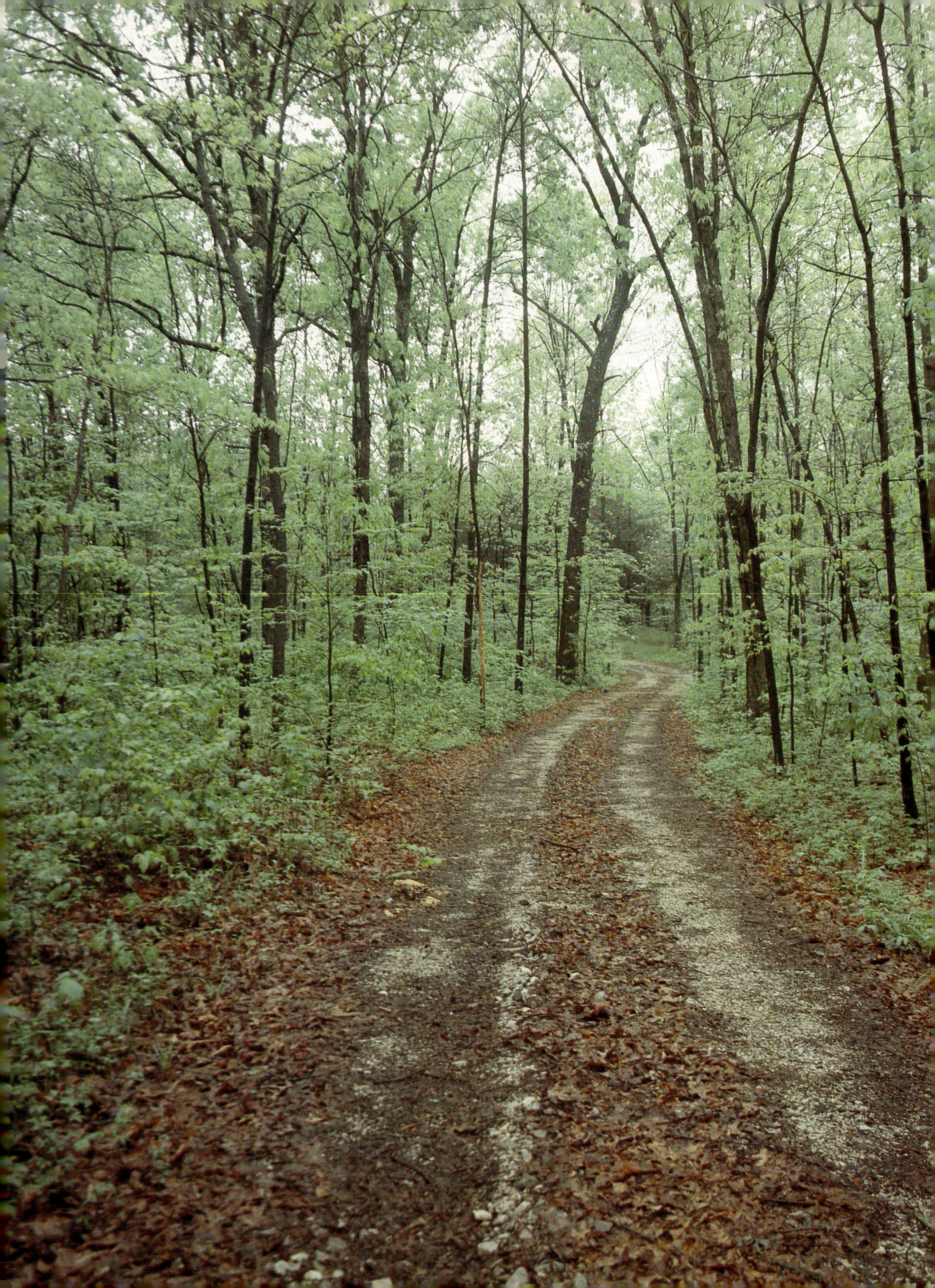

The Brown County Book

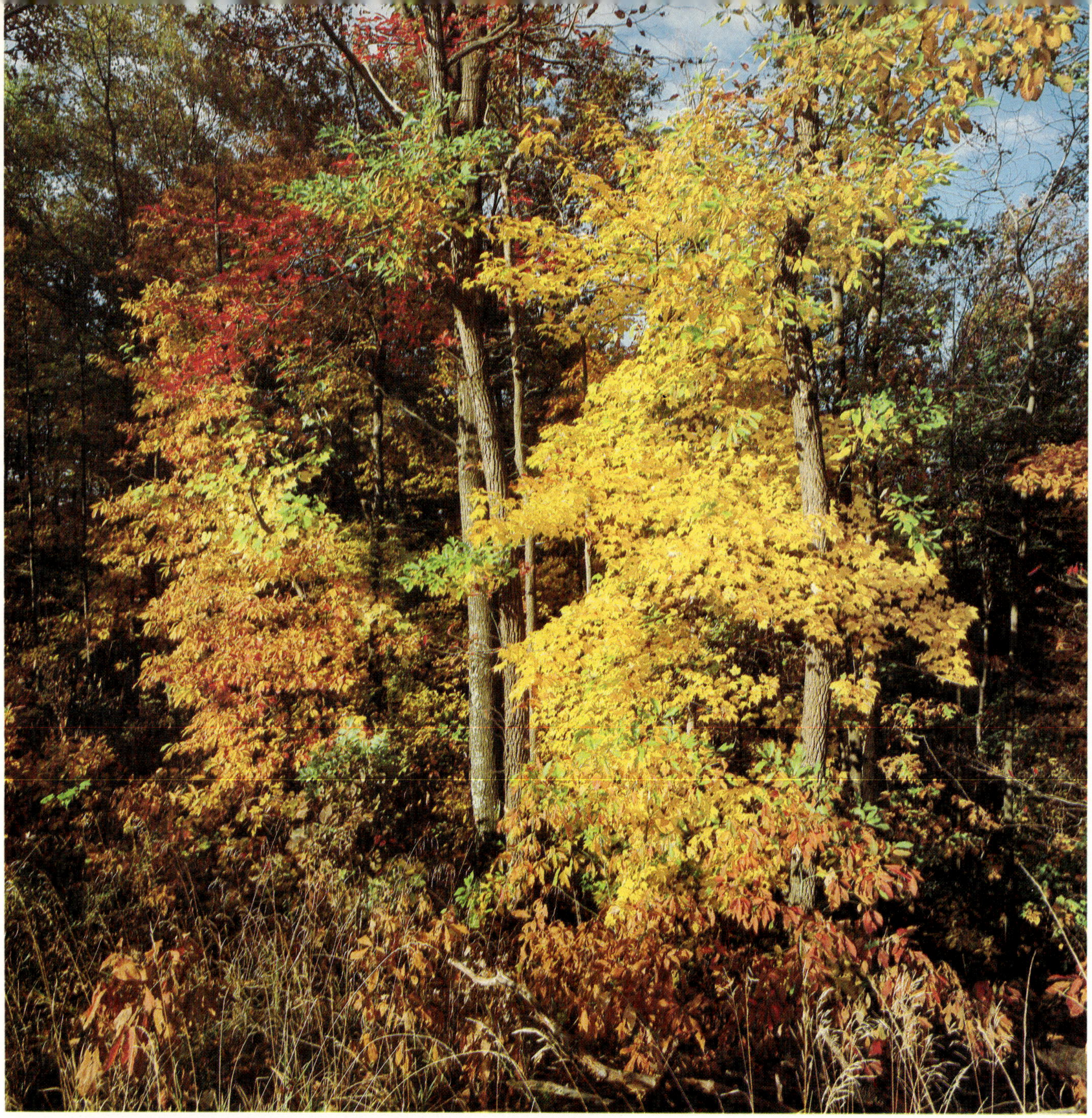

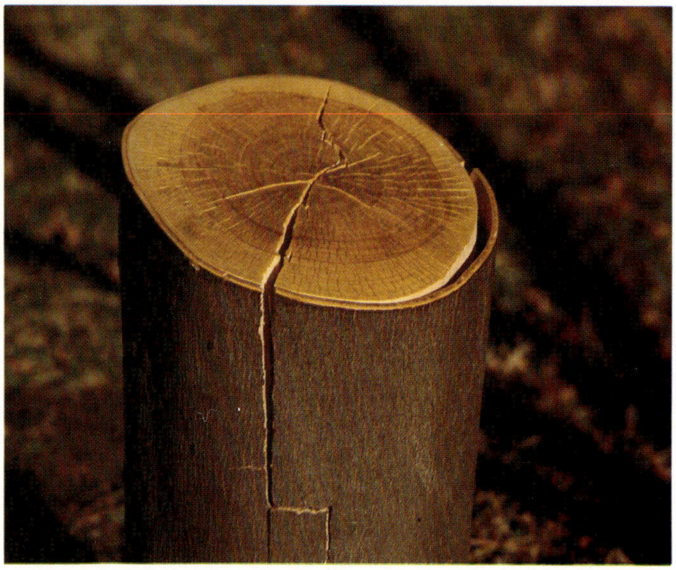

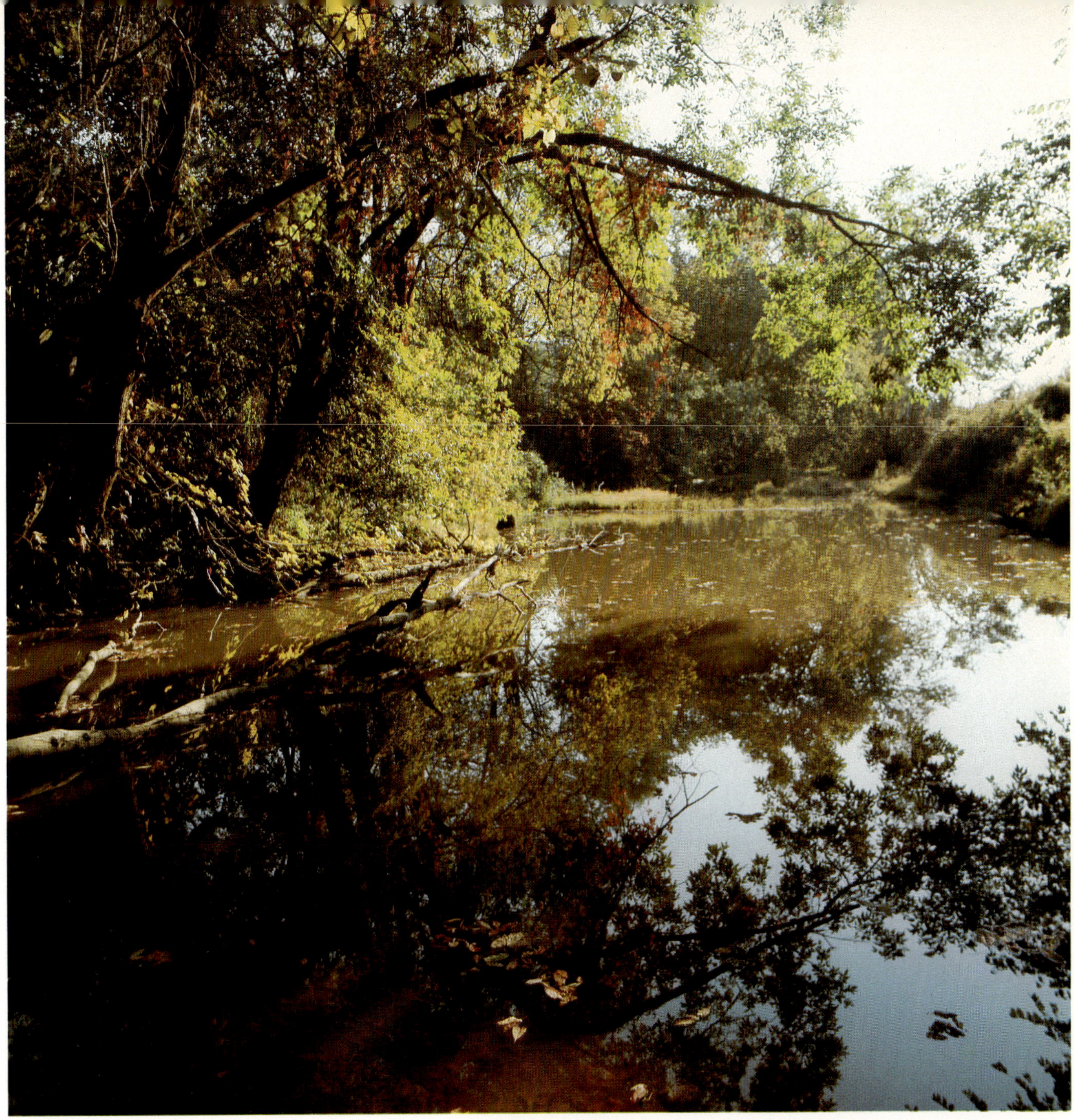

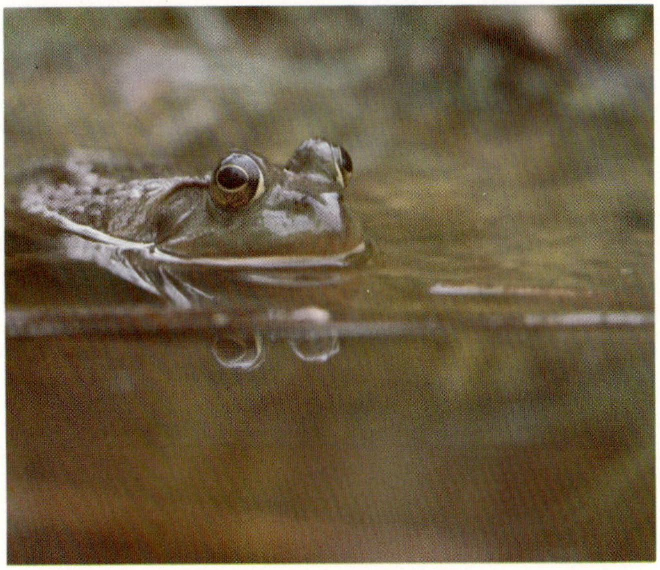

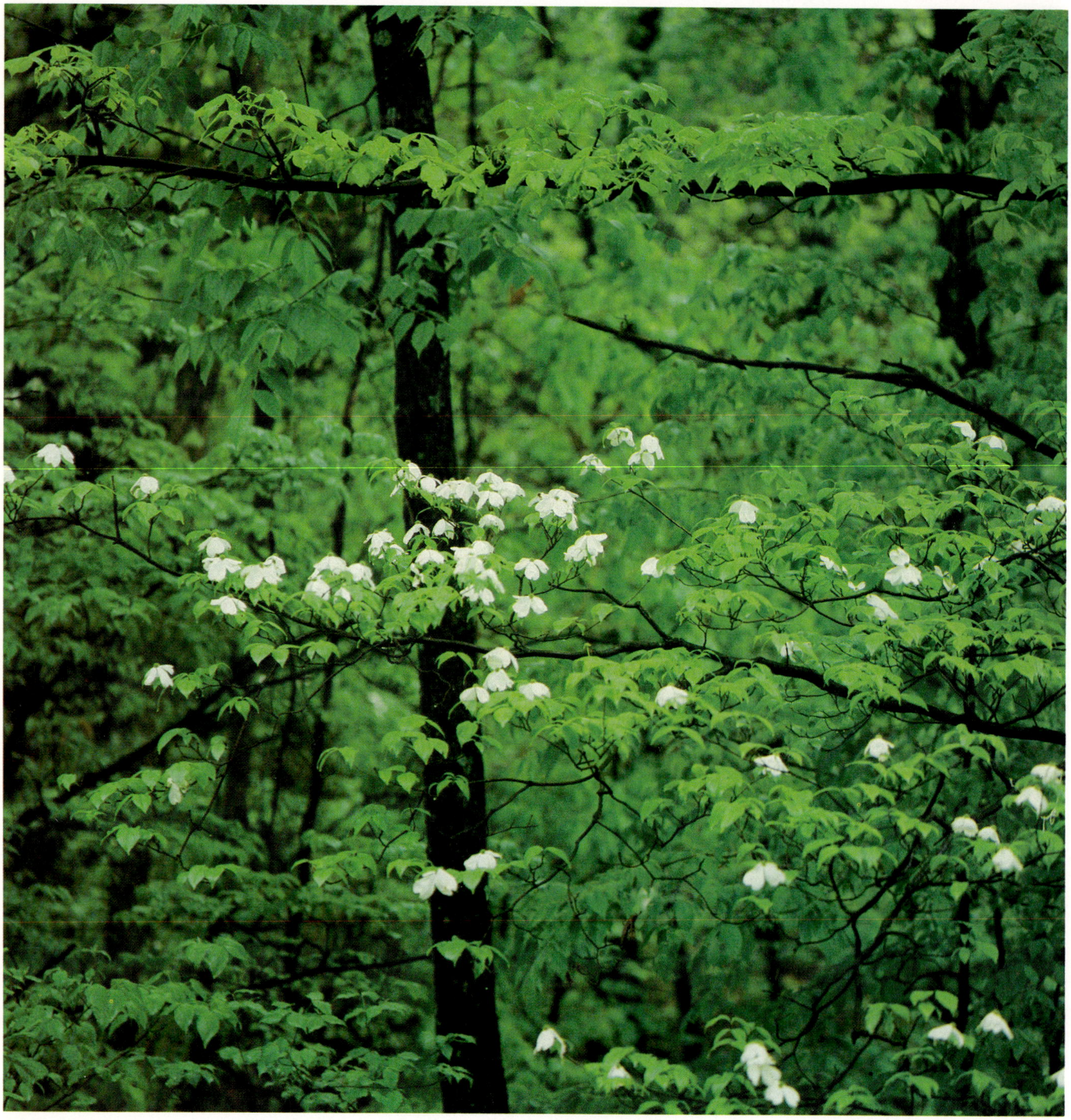

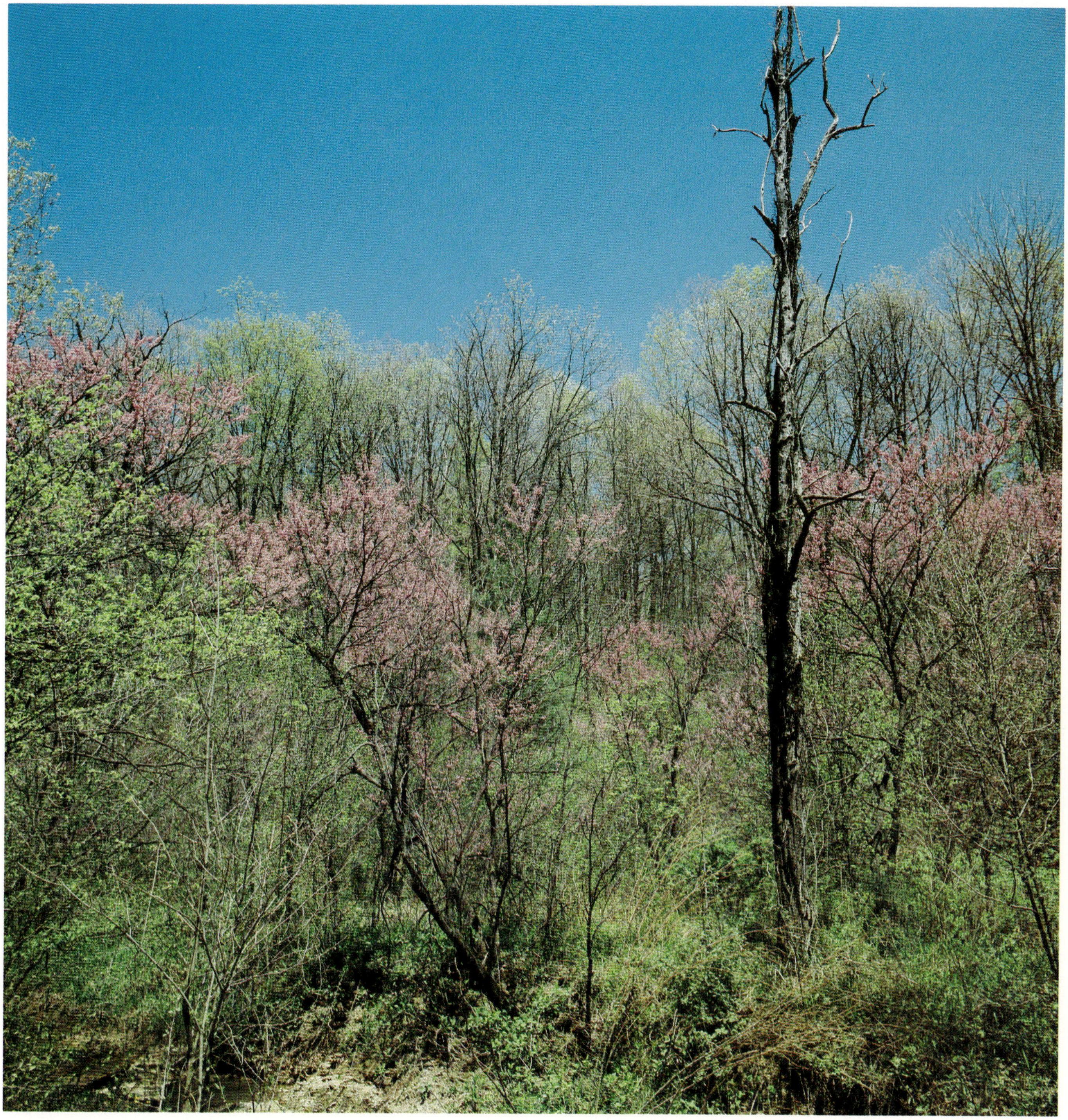

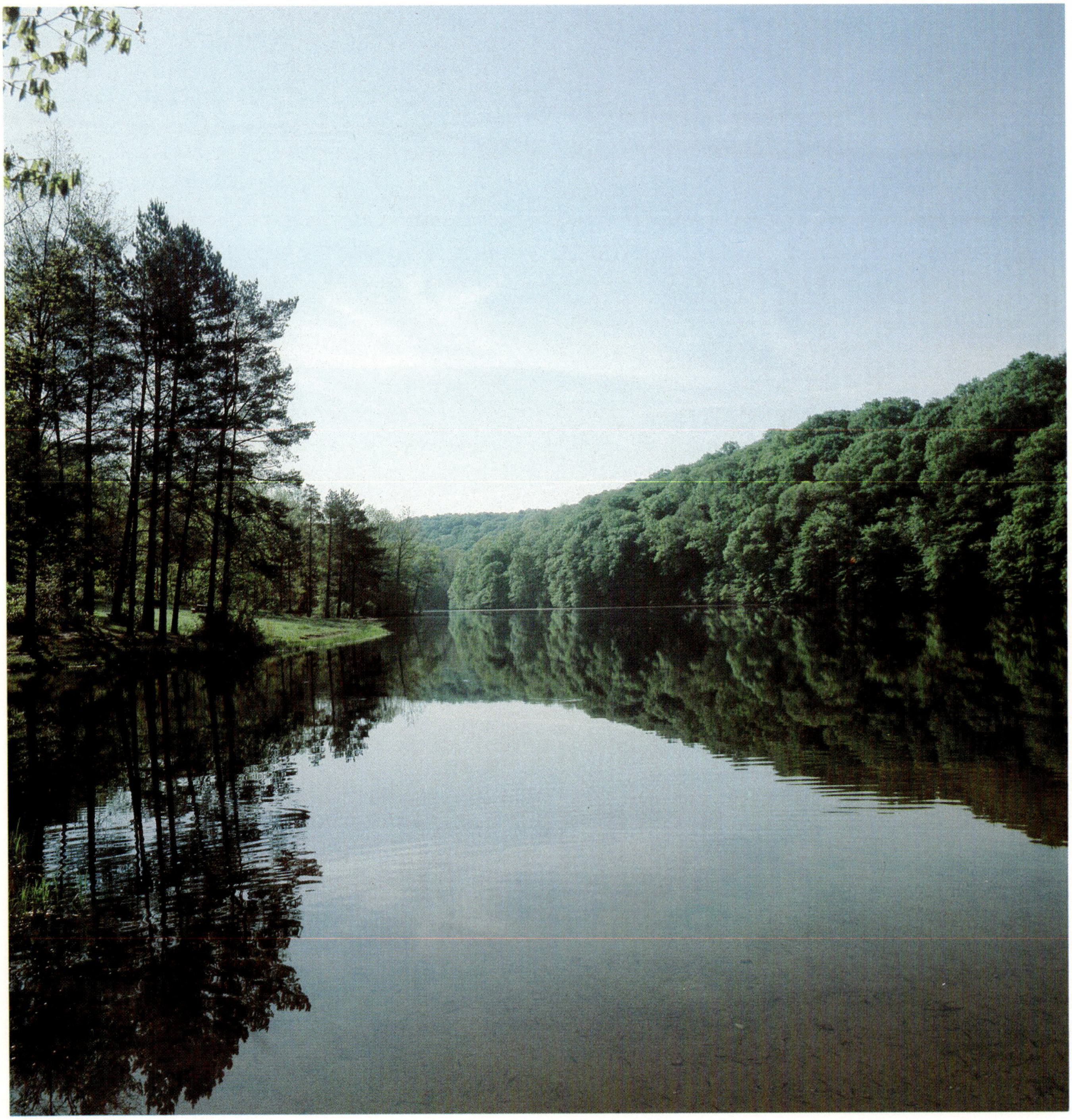

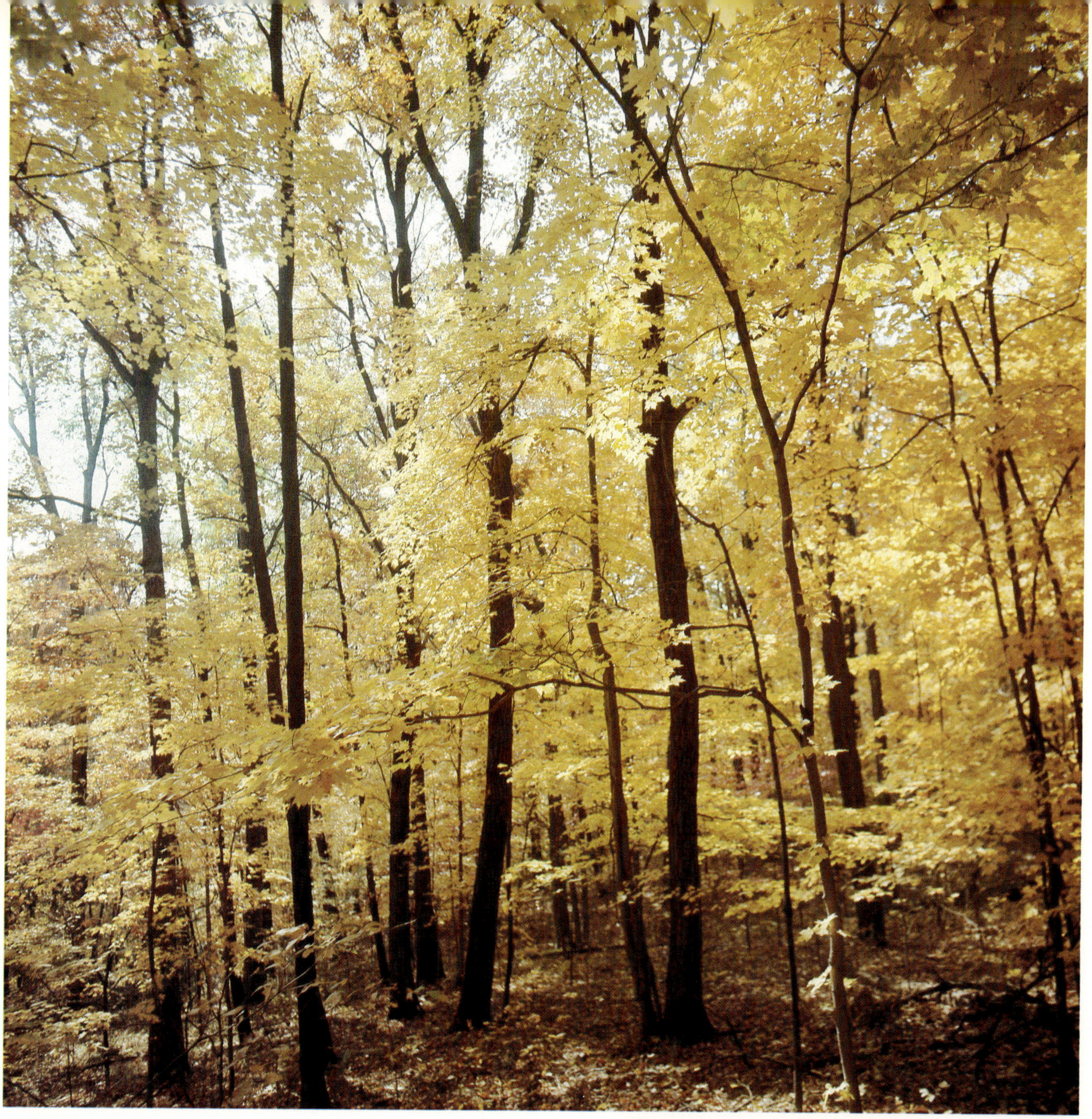
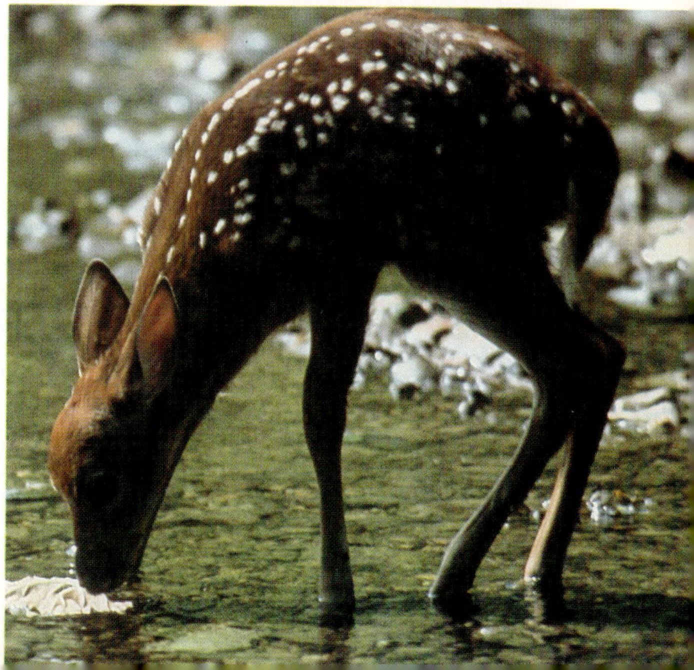

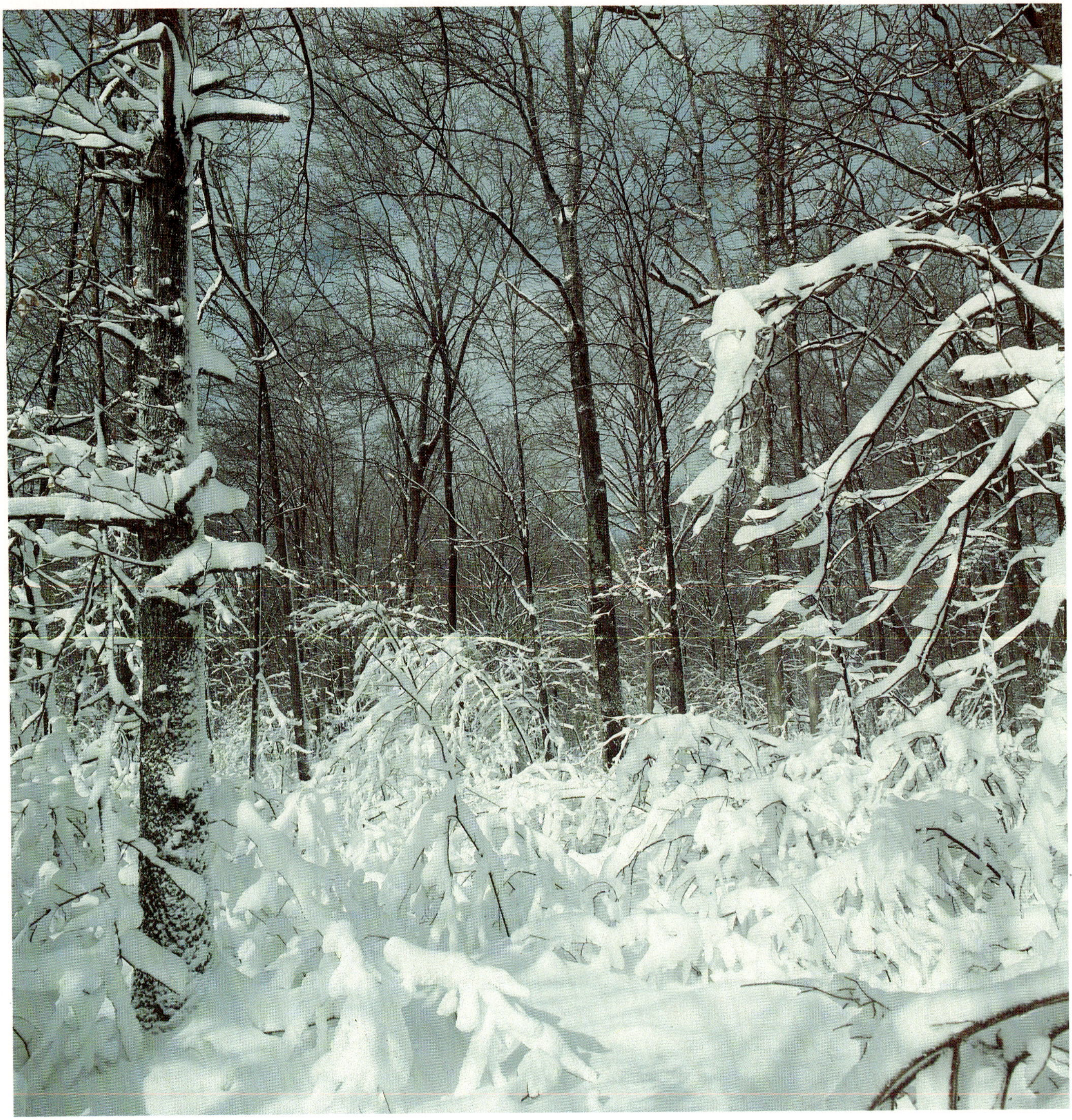

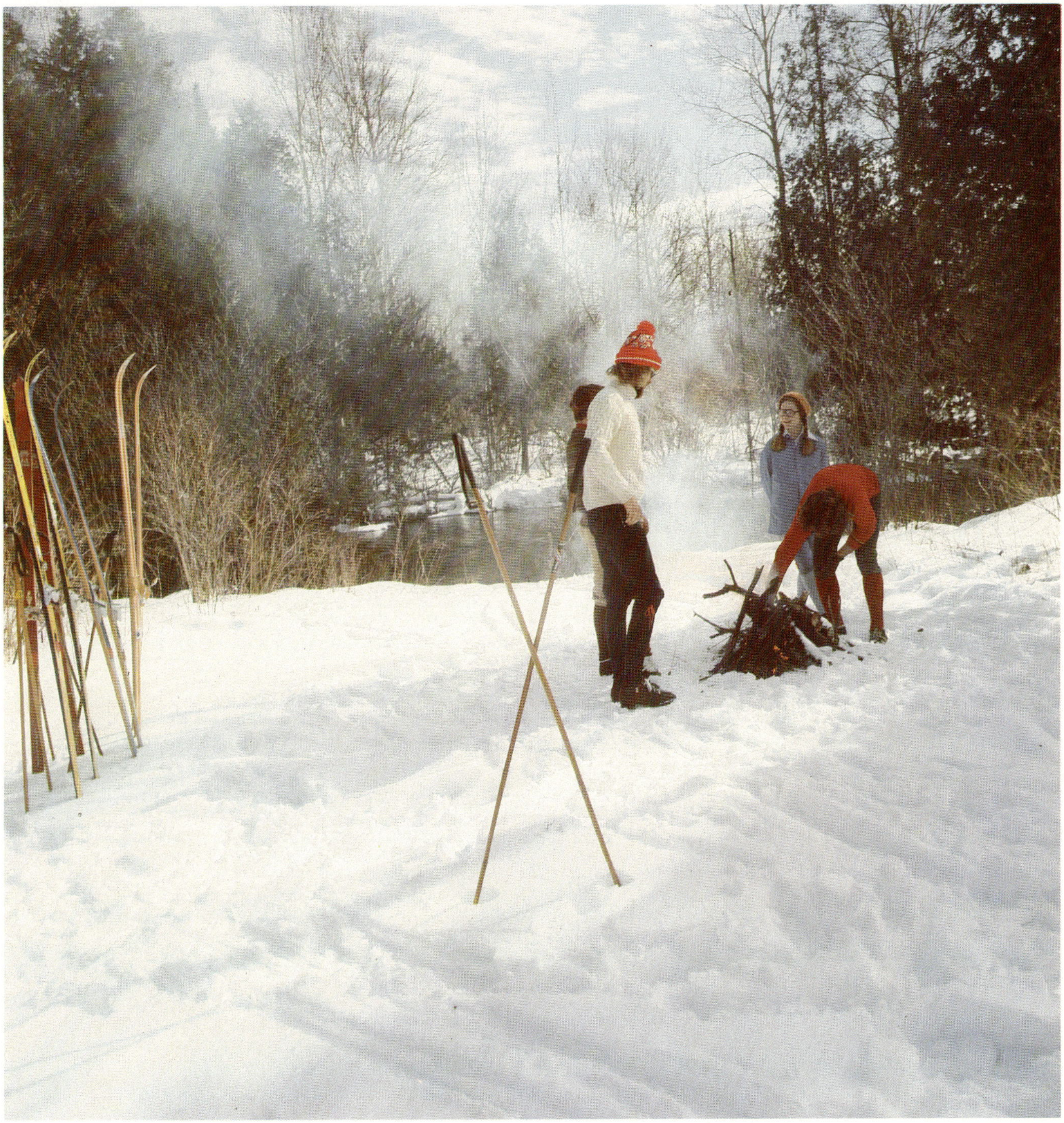

Brown County The Place

1 Brown County is a sprawling land of soft wooded hills and hollows bathed a good deal of the year in translucent blue haze. It possesses a unique character and a rustic atmosphere which attracts a great variety of people from all parts of the globe. To those who seek natural beauty, it has become a mecca, particularly in spring and fall when the rugged landscape is decorated with splashes of color. To those who seek simplicity, Brown County is also a slightly sophisticated version of Dogpatch, USA.

To satirist Kin Hubbard, who for years produced the nationally syndicated cartoon character, Abe Martin, Brown County was the setting which provided the country wit and humor the world awaited. And while many of the county's residents took issue with Hubbard, he was not far from reality in the fictionalized version of Brown County and Abe Martin's Bloom Center, which actually was the village of Nashville.

Salty characters are still to be found in Brown County. And while there has been, during recent times, a great migration of people from the outside world, the county has retained a considerable portion of the flavor which makes it still unique. The absence of class or social distinctions makes it possible for the college professor to associate with the plumber, the artisan with the woodcutter, the scientist and writer with the farmer, and for all to share, in some perspective, a common ground. Furthermore, it is, in a sense, a place of escape, and many of the people living here have either escaped to or from something.

Although basically rural in nature, the county is not one of agricultural pursuit. Only six full-time farmers are to be found, and most of those are located either in the glaciated area north of Bean Blossom Creek or along the broad stream valleys created by Salt Creek or its tributaries. There are a number of part-time farmers, but not enough to create a large impact upon farming within the county or elsewhere. And it certainly doesn't compare with agricultural production in any of the adjoining counties.

Most of the land is too poor, too rocky, too shallow, or too hilly to farm. It doesn't even make good pasture and if it did, the hillsides are so steep, one farmer said, the cows would have to have two short legs on one side to permit them to graze. A part of the Norman Upland, a great tongue of high land extending northward from the Ohio River, a good portion of the county remained untouched by the last two great glaciers. The Wisconsin glacier did extend as far south as Bean Blossom Creek, however, and evidence of it can be seen to this day. If you'll stand, for instance, at the Bean Blossom Overlook on SR 135 north of Nashville, the panorama before you was landscaped by the glacier. And the area where you're standing was not.

Pockets of unglaciated land north of Bean Blossom Creek exist, too, but they are generally small. You can recognize them by their tall steep ridges and sharp ravines with narrow streambeds, similar to those found in Brown County State Park. The area included in the park, incidentally, is acclaimed as one of the finest examples of Norman Upland territory because of those characteristic landforms. As you stand at overlooks along the periphery of Weed Patch Hill, for instance, in the state park and look at the faraway horizon, you may be impressed with how level the horizon appears, yet the landscape between you and the horizon is a series of rugged folds and distinctive ridges. That's because the entire area was at one time a plain and even prior to that the bottom of the pre-Cambrian Sea. It's from that era that many of the fossils were formed.

Generally speaking, while the northern half of the county was landscaped by the glacier, the southern half was not. And the large number of visitors come to view the great scenic beauty in the unglaciated portions where the ridges and valleys are covered by second-growth timber. A mixture of yellow poplar, oak, hickory, beech, sassafras, dogwood, maple, redbud, and elm, the trees dress themselves in autumn in a bursting display of reds and golds and shades in between. Even before the turn of the century, Brown County had become known as one of the prime fall color spots in the nation. It was this scenic beauty, coupled with the translucent blue haze, that attracted numerous artists, a number of whom later moved to the county to paint.

While there are considerable open areas in the county, most of its 207,360 acres are heavily forested. Yellowwood State Forest, portions of the Hoosier National Forest, and Brown County State Park occupy vast acreage, thereby giving the county one of its nicknames—"The Place of Trees." Their plentifulness and the lay of the land also have led many people to compare Brown County to the Great Smoky Mountains of North Carolina and Tennessee. Analogies are sometimes drawn between Nashville, the county seat and largest community in the county, and Gatlinburg, Tennessee, the center of activity for the Great Smoky Mountains. Both are very commercial.

From 1820 to 1830, the people who first settled the county migrated mostly from the Appalachians, from Kentucky to the Carolinas. A few came from Pennsylvania and Ohio. For the most part, they were rawboned, hardworking, tough, and painfully dedicated to digging out a survival for themselves from the land. The first settlement was at Elkinsville in the south central portion of the county, an area which has been steadily losing population since World War II. And now much of that area where life for the white man began in Brown County has assumed the appearance of wilderness, not greatly different in many respects from those early days of 1820. Most of the land in that part of the county is either owned by the U. S. Forest Service, the state of Indiana, or the U. S. Army Corps of Engineers, which built Lake Monroe, one of the two largest impoundments in the state. The tailwaters extend well into Brown County.

A few Indians visited the county prior to the white settler, and even thereafter—mostly Delawares and Miami from northern Indiana. But as far as can be determined, Indians viewed Brown County as a place to visit, not to live in. Remnants of Indian culture have been found along the North Fork of Salt Creek, along Gnawbone Creek, and near Bear Wallow Hill. And there are legends of Indians, mostly individuals or families, living near Story in the broad valley of the South Fork of Salt Creek and near Helmsburg and Trevlac along or near Bean Blossom Creek. So-called Indian trees, bent to grow in a certain direction, can still be found at several locations in the county. Theories persist they were groomed to grow the way they did by Indians who used them for trail guides or landmarks as they traveled through this territory.

Jack Weddle, outdoor education teacher for many years at Brown County High School and a self-proclaimed scholar of Indian culture in southern Indiana, says he has found evidence mostly of hunting camps or occasionally a lone Indian residence. "The county was unattractive to the Indian because there was nothing for him here. The stone was not good for making tools, the land was too poor on which to grow crops, the wildlife was too sparse to make it an enticing hunting ground. The mixed mesophytic forest environment normally is not ecologically suitable for wildlife habitat," he said. "In fact, it is, in one sense, a good example of nature polluting itself by applying too much acid to the soil, crowding out sustenance plants which provide food for animals and smaller creatures. And thus, the Indian found the county beautiful, as does the present visitor or dweller, but not conducive for any kind of permanent lifestyle."

The first settlers didn't find it much better, but they managed to eke out a living in what fertile lands they could find. And of course, when they moved into the county, there were vast stands of virgin timber from which they could build their homes and heat them. Enough wild game existed to provide them with meat for the table and clothes for warmth. They raised whatever else they needed. They built their homes in the shelter of the hillsides, mostly, avoiding the low places because they feared the diseases and fevers that they believed existed in such places.

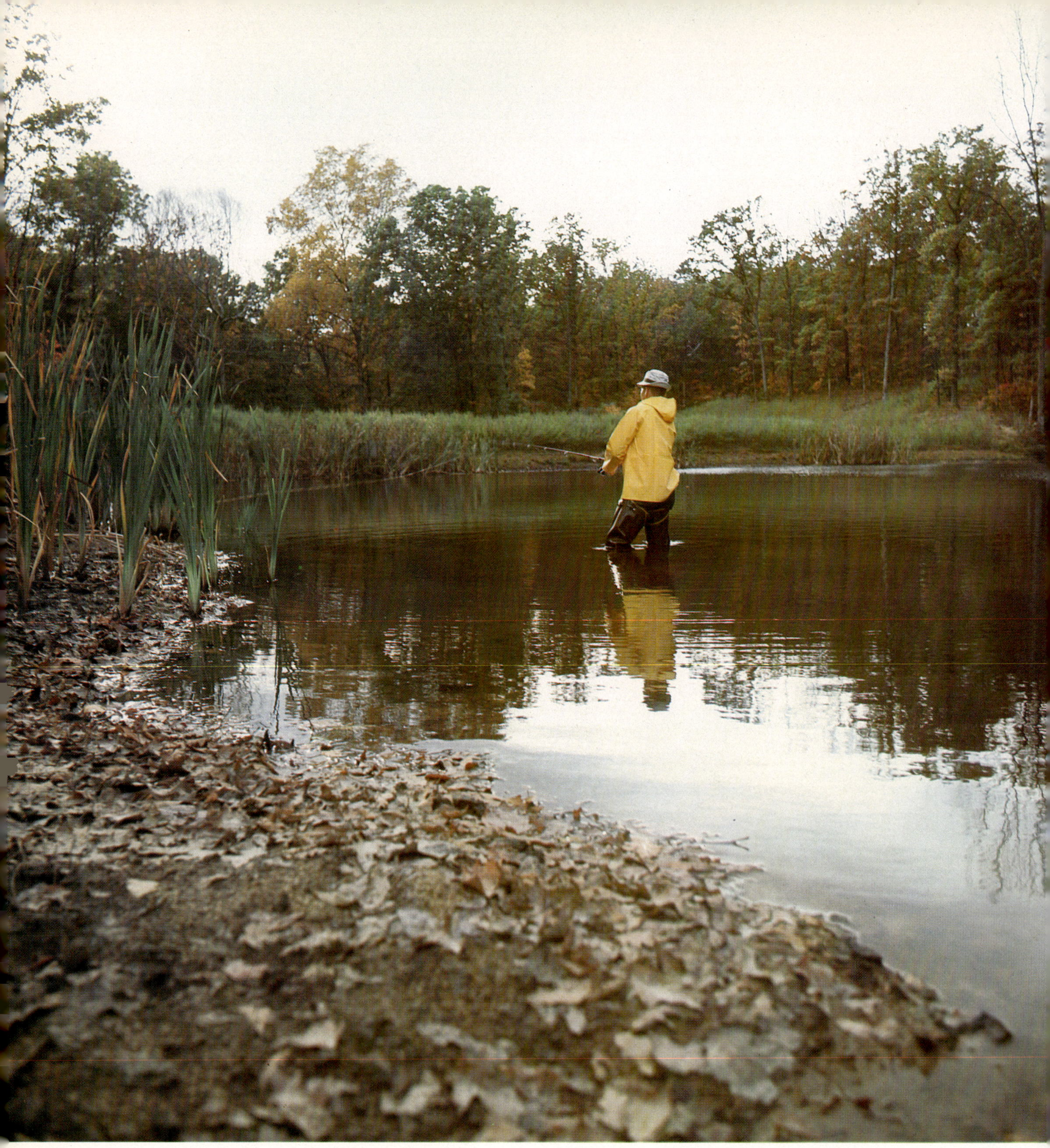

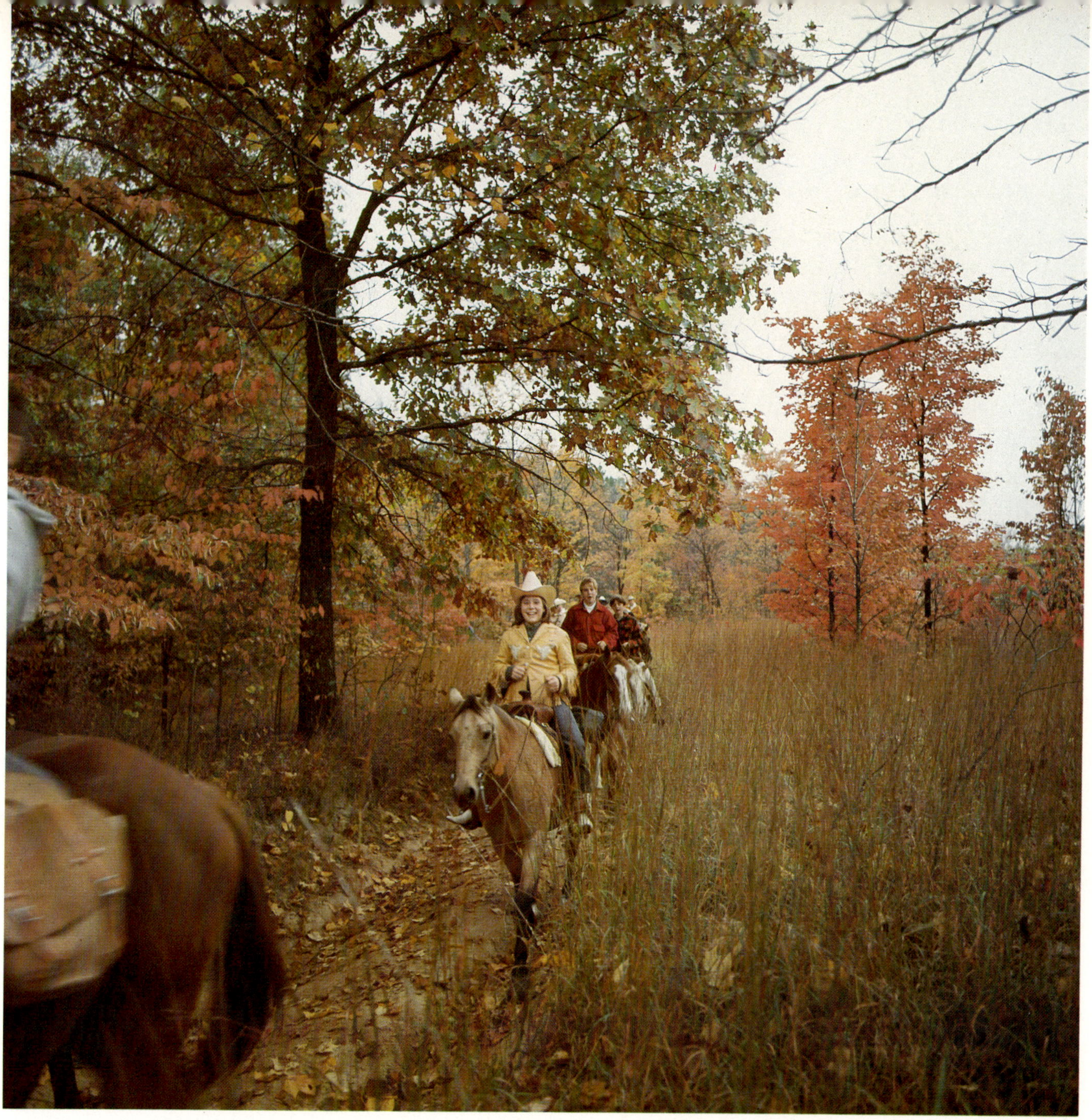

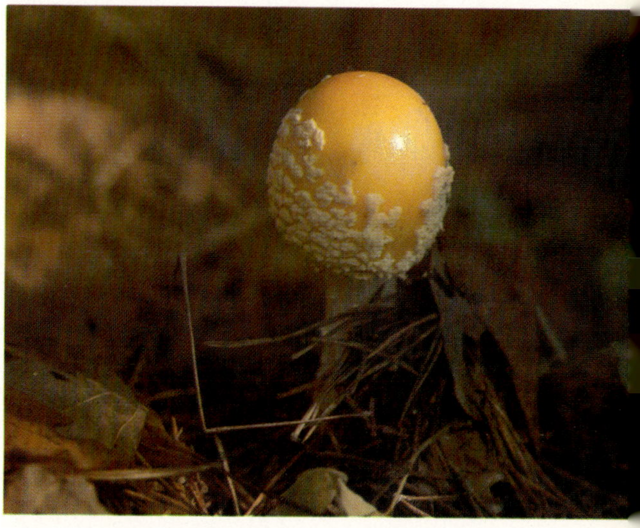

The mainstay of transportation in Brown County has always been by road, first by horse, then horse and buggy, and more currently, the automobile, but during the early days when Nashville was young, flatboats plied Salt Creek carrying goods from the county by way of the White River and ultimately the Ohio and Mississippi to New Orleans. In the period from 1830 to 1836, a flatboat dock was operated at what is now Nashville, then known as Jacksonburg, but the boats could only use the creek during high water. At that time, usually in the spring, boats loaded with grain and salt pork departed Nashville. Other flatboats were built at points downstream by Elijah Scarborough and Al Meadows. These boats, of course, were sold along with their cargo, and the crews hiked or rode horses back to the hills of Brown County.

The Illinois Central Railroad line into the county was built about 1905, and two daily trains ultimately carried passengers to and from stations at Fruitdale, Trevlac, and Helmsburg. But the first real progress in transportation came in February 1920 when SR 46 was completed, giving visitors an access from east and west. And when SR 135 was built down from Indianapolis in 1930, the Indianapolis newspapers predicted Brown County would make Indianapolis famous, giving the city a claim to beauty at its doorstep. Then in 1931–1932 SR 45 was completed, linking Bloomington to Bean Blossom and SR 135.

Although people began coming to Brown County before the turn of the century just to enjoy the scenery, it wasn't until after World War II that tourism actually began to play such a vital role in the county's economy. Prior to that time, people still relied heavily upon subsistence agriculture and timber-cutting. It was a poor, economically depressed area, to be sure, but that depression also gave it character. Even as late as 1960, Brown County was included in a discussion in *The Saturday Evening Post* entitled "The Plight of the Hill People."

Louise Kissling, who was born in a cabin where the Brown County Country Club is now located, moved away when she was still a little girl, but her parents returned regularly to visit folks they had known in Brown County. And she remembers spending weekends here. "You couldn't believe how poor the people were," she recalls. "But they were hospitable and would do anything in the world for you. They ate simply and lived simply. Their cabins had no screens on the windows or doors, and there was no electricity or telephone. Most of them had no automobiles, but traveled instead by horse and buggy or wagon, or walked. The roads were gravel or just dirt, rough, filled with chuckholes, narrow and winding. But it was beautiful, more beautiful than it is today because there were so few people and there were so few houses."

Had it not been for just three persons, however, two of whom moved to Brown County, the future of the area might have been an entirely different story. For those three—artist T. C. Steele, photographer Frank Hohenberger, and political satirist Kin Hubbard—had profound impact in putting Brown County on the map.

The scenic beauty enticed Steele to move here and paint landscapes he sold to people all over the country, but it was a combination of scenic beauty and the hill people that inspired Hohenberger. And Hubbard was attracted to the people and the culture of the place. As a result of their combined creative activity, Brown County became known in all parts of North America as well as in some parts of Europe.

The grass-roots lifestyle of the people helped to maintain a colorful atmosphere, however. That atmosphere bred old sayings, superstitions, place names, and food recipes that were unusual. Many of the handicrafts that were passed down from generation to generation during the pioneer days as a matter of necessity remained intact in Brown County for that same reason. The county did not progress with other areas. Instead it remained secluded and off the beaten track. And the crafts and character were retained.

Among the local color were the place names. Gnawbone, of course, is perhaps the most unusual, but there are Bean Blossom, Bear Wallow, Fruitdale, Pike's Peak, Needmore, Scarce O'Fat Ridge, Starve Hollow, Booger Hollow, Possum Trot Road, Milk Sick Bottom, Owl Creek, Stone Head, Story, and Greasy Creek. On the western side of the county, a town was to be named after a fellow named Calvert, but since there already was a Calvert, Indiana, it was decided the town name should be Calvert spelled backwards. And it became Trevlac. There ought, by all means, to be a Dogpatch.

An old farm wagon on Greasy Creek Ro

Although the names are colorful, few of the stories behind the names are. In fact, it's debatable in most instances just how some place names came to be. Gnawbone, for instance, has a half dozen or more explanations, the most intriguing one being it was named by a Frenchman who called it Narbonne. The people colloquialized it, and the name became Gnawbone. But it's probably not true. Another version is that a company of Union soldiers came through during the Civil War and stopped to eat here. One got drunk, and they left him sitting beside the road gnawing on a bone left over from lunch. Still a third version has it one of the owners of the mill located in the town would not care for his horses, and they kept dying off. And dogs fed upon the bones. For many months, passersby would notice dogs lying around gnawing on bones and thus the place was so named.

At the highest point in Brown County State Park is Weed Patch Hill, so named because it was a natural opening as long as people can remember, a kind of hilltop prairie. And it seemed weeds grew profusely there. Used to be a little town with a post office atop Weed Patch Hill; it was called Kelp, after an old Brown County family, descendants of whom still live in the county.

Bear Wallow Hill was originally called Teepee Mountain by the Indians, according to Indian legendeer Jack Weddle. The good spirit was supposed to dwell there, and it was considered a sacred place. Black bears came there to wallow in water holes during hot weather. Because of the wallowing, the holes became larger, and thus the name.

Pike's Peak was so named when a man from Ohio during the great westward movement set out in a covered wagon for Pike's Peak, Colorado. Tired of traveling and plagued with problems with his wagon, he refused to be discouraged, however, and in his efforts to rationalize, chose a tall hill, built a cabin and staked a claim to the land, calling it Pike's Peak.

Booger Hollow was named after a shoe salesman who disappeared there during the early days of the county. Folks thought a ghost had kidnapped him.

And Bean Blossom was named for the creek by the same name, flowing just south of town. It originally was called Georgetown.

Needmore was named because someone described the folks living there as being so poor, they needed more of everything.

Changes were slow in Brown County; for years, it did not keep pace with the rest of the world, and it was that difference that gave it appeal. The good ol' days people wistfully remembered in other places still flourished in Brown County. Even during the 1950s, electricity still had not come to many rural homes in the area; neither had indoor plumbing. Telephones were few and far between. The roads were narrow and winding; many of them still are.

Hohenberger in his diary once commented: "A lady from Florida who has spent time in Canada where they have perfectly straight roads remarked that a snake would break its back traveling over our winding thoroughfares. I told her if we straightened them out we wouldn't have room for all of them."

But times are changing in Brown County. The old breed which once occupied the liars' bench on the county courthouse lawn is disappearing. The country store atmosphere is virtually gone. And in its place have come new spiffy shops with prices to match. Some say the county is doomed, that Nashville has become so commercial soon no one will come here, and many of the old-time natives wonder why people do. But the people do continue to come. Year after year, the crowds grow larger, the traffic on the main highways heavier and heavier. It's now necessary to have two traffic lights in Nashville, and it was only after a great deal of discussion and some controversy that even the first one was installed just a few years ago.

Major lodges and tourist resorts in the county, particularly in Nashville, are often booked up for months in advance and, during the autumn season, a year in advance. Two ski resorts are the latest additions to the county's economic picture, opening up still another season for visitors. And Nashville, which used to be a sleepy little village during the winter months, now thrives the year round. The first Winter Festival, held during the 1979–80 season, drew crowds far beyond expectation.

True, the new image and the new day has brought about many changes and virtually a disappearance of the lifestyle that made Brown County famous. The fried biscuits, sassafras tea, baked apple butter, red-eye gravy, and ham steaks are still major items of cuisine hereabouts, but somehow the flavor is not quite the same as in the olden days when such giants as T. C. Steele and his companions painted along the roadsides, when Hohenberger published his photographs nationwide in magazines, or when Kin Hubbard created his cartoon character Abe Martin of Brown County for the *Indianapolis News*. It was a grand day when Abe Martin, Professor Alex Tansey, Miss Fawn Lippincutt, young Lafe Bud, Constable Newt Plum, and Miss Germ Williams came to town.

Since that time, however, publicity has not been necessary. Each autumn the main throng of visitors comes, publicity or not. The months of September, October, and November witness the county's population multiply twenty-five times as traffic on the highways stacks up bumper to bumper. On weekends, most residents give up going anywhere unless it's an absolute necessity. At times, I've waited for thirty minutes at the end of my gravel road for a break in the traffic to allow me to pull onto SR 46.

25

Flea markets, roadside stands selling homegrown pumpkins, fruits, vegetables, honey, black walnut candy, antiques, paintings and drawings and etchings do a booming business all over the county. Peak tourist weekend coincides most of the time with peak fall color, and upwards of 175,000 cars drive through Brown County during that time. The fact that gasoline prices soared to more than $1 per gallon made absolutely no difference; the numbers of tourists coming to the county steadily grows each year.

Spring is the second largest tourist season, when the redbud and dogwood are in bloom. It's also the time when there's just enough color to accentuate the county's dwellings, but not enough to hide them as the thick foliage often does later in the summer. The annual log cabin tour is one of the county's most popular events. And there are a number of log cabins located all over the county. Even Nashville has more than 50, and there may be as many as 450 or more outside Nashville in other parts of the county. The oldest—the Brummett cabin—is located in Nashville, and the Kelley cabin atop Kelley Hill near the west entrance to the state park dates back to 1840. While a good number of log cabins go back to the early part of this century, not all of them are old. New ones are continually being built, some of them considerably larger than cabins, and split rail fences, which became a trademark of the county, still are being done. So some of the flavor of yesteryear is being retained.

While earlier-day migrants came from the southeast, latter-day ones come from everywhere, giving the county a cosmopolitan mixture. It's not unusual during the course of a single day while traveling around the area to meet folks who moved from Detroit, Chicago, New York City, Baltimore, Boston, parts of California, Texas, or the Pacific Northwest. Some are from other countries—Germany, Scandinavia, Canada, England, and Mexico. A good number of the teaching staff at Indiana University live in Brown County, commuting daily to work. Other people commute to Columbus or Indianapolis, an hour or two to the north, depending upon which section of the county you live in.

Few people who live in the county make their living here. And if the lifestyle and quality of life that attracts people to the area are to be maintained, it must remain that way. Cabin industries make up the main thrust of production in the county; others are employed mainly with tourist-related activities, in restaurants, lodges and motor inns, and curio shops. Take away the tourism, and there's little left in Brown County for people to do. The other essential elements include some farming, timber-cutting, and activities of the county's producing artists and craftsmen.

Simplicity has been one of the main attractions for people, however, rather than employment or money. As one relocated New Yorker said: "Life here in the wooded hills is stripped to the basic elements, and there's no pretense. You are what you are, and people accept you at face value. I haven't seen any evidence whatsoever of that old idiom of keeping up with the Joneses."

Combined with simplicity is the slow pace of life. It's a cardinal sin for anyone living in the county to get in a hurry. There are few schedules to follow, and if there is one, it's regarded lightly, a reality many newcomers find difficult to live with, but it's a pace of life they must adjust to or find themselves eternally frustrated because of it.

When I first moved to Brown County several years ago, my refrigerator went on the blink. The only repairman I could find locally was an old farmer who repaired "frigs" on the side. Two days after I called him, he came, got down on his hands and knees, and looked it over carefully and decided the problem was a simple one. It merely needed some juice, he said. But instead of adding the freon, he lit up a cigarette and stood around talking for an hour. My wife had made the mistake of offering him a cup of coffee, too. I was anxious to get back to my work, but it was still another hour before the job was completed and another thirty to forty-five minutes before he finally got his tools gathered into his old pickup truck and began to back out the driveway.

"How much do I owe you?" I shouted.

He paused, rubbed his chin as though studying the matter, then squinted at me. "Oh, send me a couple of bucks," he said.

An old plow rusting in a farmer's field.

A second factor which gives the county great appeal is seclusion and the opportunity to commune with wildlife. A number of people come to live in Brown County because of this factor. As a result, more than half of the privately owned land in the county is posted against hunting, fishing, or trespassing in any form. Brown County is, after all, one of the few places where the landowner can, in a sense, close off the rest of the world. And most of those who live here hold a great respect and admiration for wildlife. Abe Eyed, who moved a few years ago from Indianapolis to Brown County and is active in the Sassafras Chapter of the Audubon Society, said: "You'll undoubtedly find more bird-lovers in Brown County than any other county in the United States." Many others are just as protective of other types of wildlife—the herds of white-tailed deer that roam the county, the raccoon, opossum, skunk, wild turkey, fox, or bobcat.

A short time after my family and I moved here, we followed the practice of others and turned the wooded tract on which we live into a protected wildlife sanctuary, sternly turning away hunters and fishermen. The wildlife became our friends and added immensely to our quality of life. It is a cherished morning when we can arise to the chorus of bullfrogs and spring peepers during the early spring and summer, or watch from our deck the antics of wood ducks and mallards on the pond in front of the house. Occasionally we've watched mother deer bring their fawns to drink, turtles clamber on the logs, and snakes chase frogs virtually to our door. Blue jays, chipmunks, grouse, grosbeaks, cardinals, pileated woodpeckers, owls, and red-tailed hawks explore the woodland just feet from our house.

Because the fish are not afraid of us, they nibble at us when we swim, and inches away from our faces, they peer at us when we are snorkeling, as we search the cattails for whatever of interest we can find.

The backwoods and seclusion are not all the county has to offer, by far. It also possesses a degree of sophisticated culture, particularly in view of its proximity to Indiana University, which imports noted speakers, entertainers, artists, and scientists in a number of fields to the campus. Plays are staged at the Brown County Playhouse by the university drama department throughout the summer and fall season. Opera of a caliber near to that enjoyed at New York's Metropolitan and performed at the university's Musical Arts Center in Bloomington can be heard by Brown Countians with little more effort than it takes to attend the Little Nashville Opry to listen to such noted country entertainers as Roy Clark, Mel Tillis, or Loretta Lynn performing from the stage of a converted horse barn in Green Valley.

At Bean Blossom each spring Bill Monroe, the father of Bluegrass music, comes to town in his big air-conditioned bus to pack in a crowd for the Bluegrass Festival on the wooded grounds of the Brown County Jamboree. His sister and a brother, Birch, live at Martinsville in adjoining Morgan County. Bluegrass fans come from Brown County and throughout the nation and Canada and even Japan to spend a few days camped out in the woods listening to round-the-clock fiddling and picking. It is one of many reasons folks like to come to Brown County.

Others come for a variety of reasons. Some of them come to search for antiques. Some of the largest accumulations of fine antiques in the Midwest are to be found here. Art? Yes, many artists open their studios to visitors, allowing them to watch them work . . . and to buy a painting before they leave. Crafts? Hundreds of craft items are on sale in the myriad shops of Nashville and other points in the county, many by local craftsmen. Food? The cuisine is country style. Scenery? Brown County ranks among the top fall foliage spots in the entire Midwest, and spring is not bad, either. Backwoods culture? Available, but few visitors ever take the time or have the knowhow for searching it out.

Brown County is, indeed, many things to many people. It's that variety which continues to make it interesting.

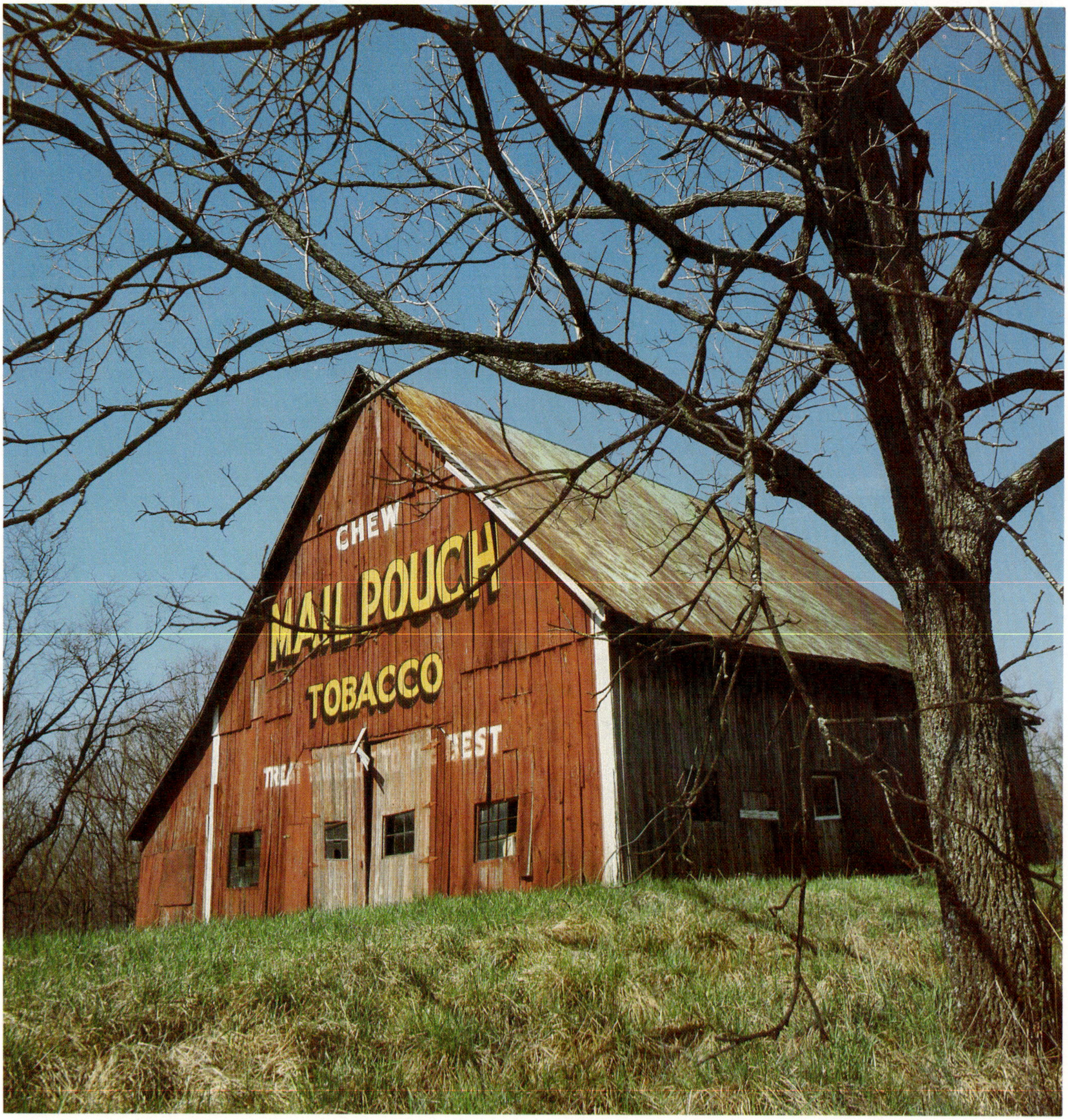
CHEW
MAIL POUCH
TOBACCO

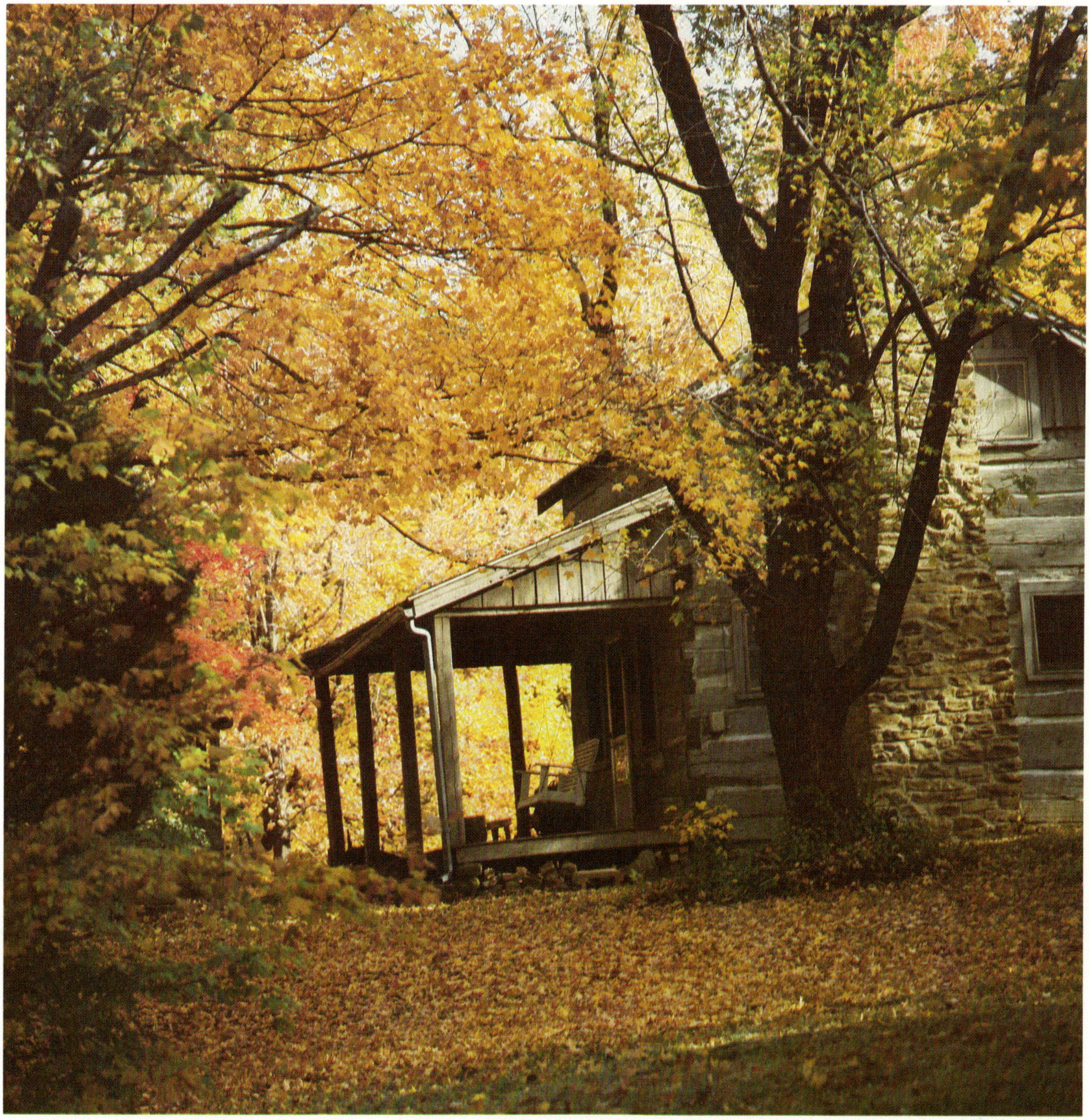

A favorite roosting place of turkey vultures is this tree along Salt Creek on the Wilbur Followell farm.

Kenny Roberts' sorghum mill at Gnaw Bone on SR 46 east.

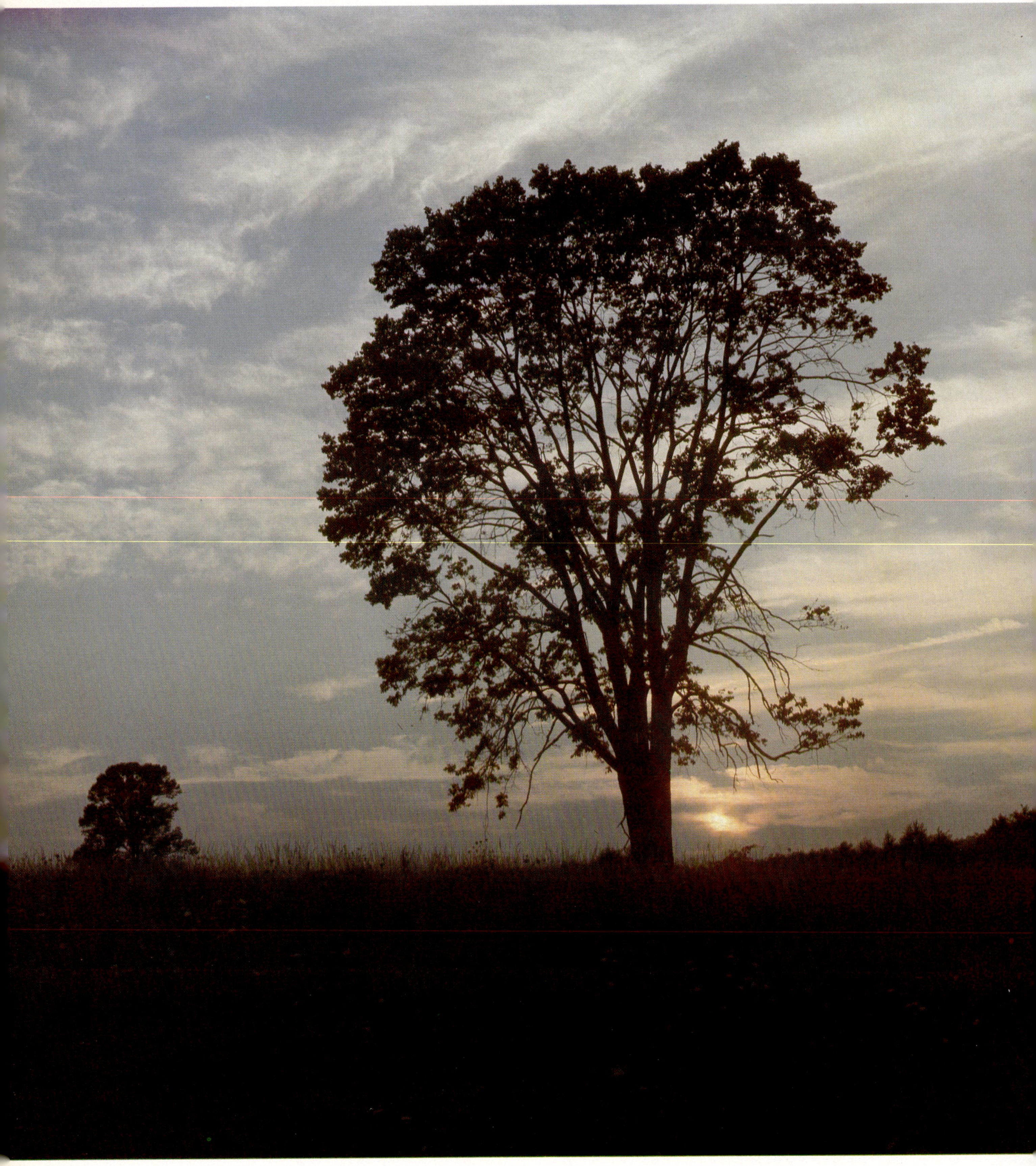

A street in downtown Nashville.

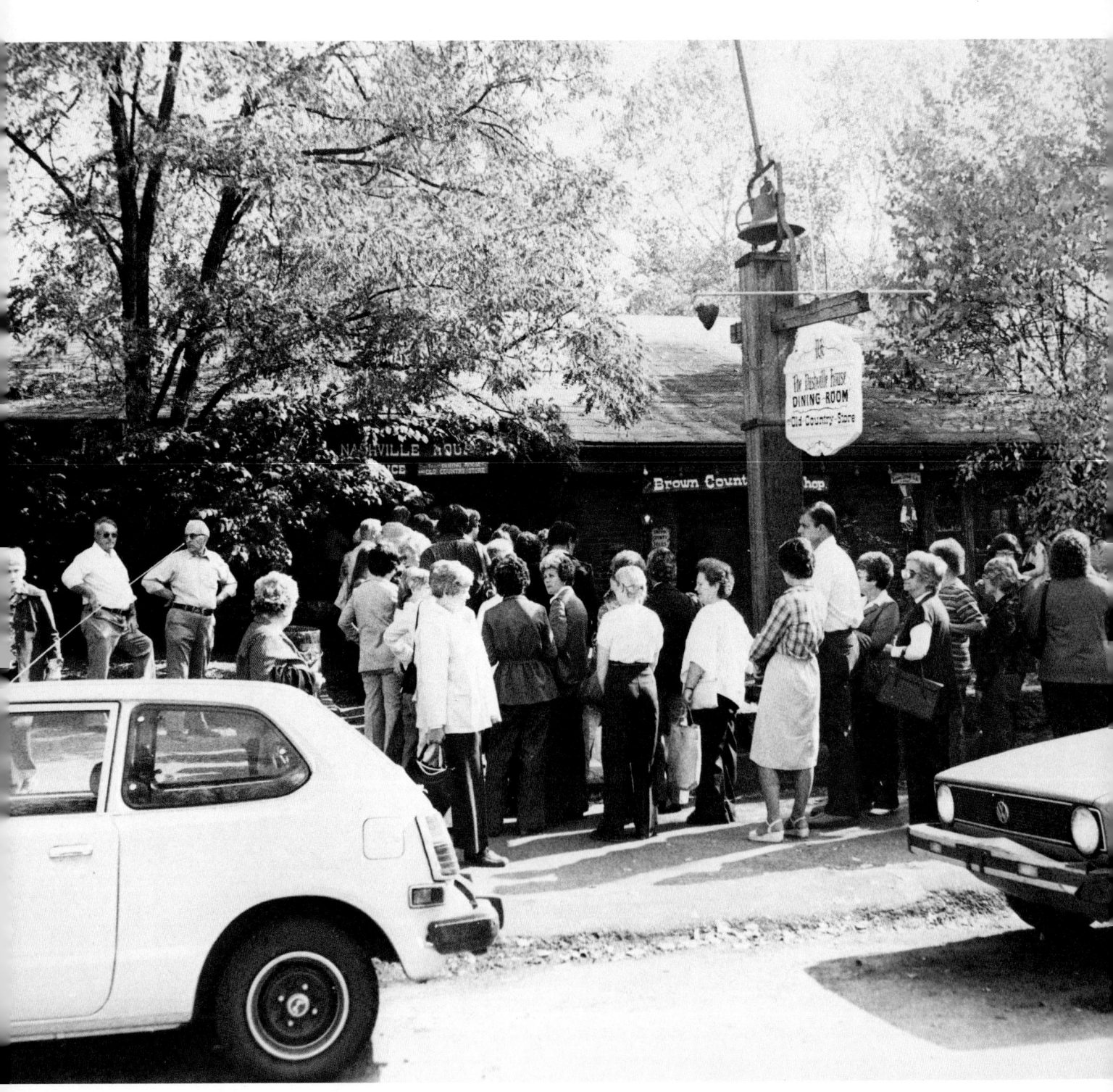

People waiting in line to eat at the Nashville House. *(Barbara Sheehan*

The Old Ferguson House in Nashville is a favorite browsing place.

Antique junk is offered the year round.

Many Brown Countians post their land, using all types of signs. This sign near Elkinsville indicates a landowner's displeasure at outside intruders.

The Mt. Zion Church and Cemetery on SR 135 south.

Bean Blossom Covered Bridge once carried the traffic on old SR 135 across Bean Blossom Creek.

A family of Canada geese on the Phil Desch farm

The Three Giants

Kin Hubbard

2 For more than a quarter of a century, a colorful, witty character named Abe Martin and his small family of friends and acquaintances made Brown County one of the best-known spots in America. Just how popular Abe Martin of Brown County was on the national scene is pointed up by a story about a time that Frank McKinney Hubbard attended a performance of the Ziegfeld Follies at the New Amsterdam Theater in New York City. Will Rogers, the comedian with the show, often introduced prominent people in the audience, and when he saw his old friend, Kin Hubbard, he asked him to stand up.

"Meet Kin Hubbard," he said, and the audience gave polite applause.

But then Rogers went on to say, "Kin Hubbard, the man who created Abe Martin of Brown County," and the audience leaped to its feet and yelled with delight. Many had never heard Kin's name, of course, but they all knew Abe Martin. Kin bowed and sat down, but the crowd was not satisfied and the applause grew still louder until he got up and bowed again. He was the hit of the show. Never in the days when he wanted to be an actor had he dreamed of having an audience so completely at his feet.

Hubbard's creation, Abe Martin, made his debut in the *Indianapolis News* in 1904, shortly after Kin, as political cartoonist, had been to Brown County accompanying a political campaigner. He was impressed by what he saw and the people he met. And although he began the cartoon with a setting elsewhere, less than three months later, Abe up and announced one day he's moving "ter Brown County ter stay." With that, he loaded up his one-horse wagon with all his earthly belongings and with a quip, "By cracky, it's sum travelin' ter git to Brown County," left the city forever.

Just five years later, Abe became nationally syndicated, running in more than 300 newspapers daily, and was reprinted in Great Britain and parts of Europe. Everyone knew Brown County through Abe Martin, for it was a popular cartoon. It drew the attention and acclaim of the greats and near greats around the country.

Herbert Hill, the illustrious editor of *Outdoor Indiana* magazine, was a cub reporter whose desk backed up to Kin Hubbard's at the *Indianapolis News;* they came to be good friends and Hill is perhaps the best living expert on Hubbard and Abe Martin. Hill often likes to relate the story of the constant procession of dignitaries, literary agents, theatrical greats, and nationally known politicians who came to visit Kin Hubbard. One of the most frequent visitors was Will Rogers, who often proclaimed Hubbard as the world's leading humorist.

"There was never a dull moment in the office during those days," Hill recalls. "Hubbard was shy, sensitive, and soft spoken, but he possessed great clout and made a profound impact upon people wherever he went."

Once Hubbard, returning from a sporting event at Indiana University in Bloomington by way of Brown County, had to stop to get water for his thirsty car at a Nashville service station. Few people in Brown County knew him, but they knew Abe Martin. And many took the character personally, as well as some of Hubbard's other creations. On this day, the story goes, Hubbard made the mistake of telling someone his name and he was nearly ridden out of the county on a rail.

While most Brown Countians considered Hubbard's characters and witty sayings as just good fun, others considered them an insult. Upon more than one occasion during the pursuit of field research for this book, I've personally run across several people who had little good to say about Hubbard or Abe Martin.

One man we shall leave unidentified said: "He used the good people of Brown County. Insulted them. I don't think any of us were as backward as Kin Hubbard would make us sound. And we didn't talk quite that corny, either."

Corny or not, the whimsical quips and witty sayings of Abe Martin and other characters of the Hubbard clan have proven timeless and just as apropos today as they were fifty years ago. And they're likely to remain so for a long time to come. The very reason Hubbard selected Brown County, of course, is because it lent itself well to the type of self-styled independent, if somewhat eccentric, characters he wished to portray. Probably few other places would have worked as well. Kentucky's Appalachia might have done so, in a pinch, but it lacked the culture and spirit that already had come to be associated with Brown County. The country wit belonged here, and thus Kin Hubbard capitalized upon it.

Although the name of Abe Martin is fairly well known here (after all, there's the Abe Martin Lodge in the state park and the Abe Martin Realty), the cast of characters that Kin Hubbard created, all of them a part of his Brown County community, are little known by contemporary society. Here is Hubbard's own rundown of some of the neighbors and friends which made up the Abe Martin circle of satire that he produced until his death in 1930.

"ABE MARTIN was born at Roundhead, Hardin County, Ohio, sometime between the first and second Seminole Wars. He got his early education in a printing office and played a yellow clarinet in a band of Johnson's Island, Lake Erie, during the rebellion. After leaving the service he moved to Brown County, where he has since lived with his wife's folks. Mr. Martin votes the Democratic ticket for nothing and doesn't owe any money or belong to any lodges. . . . Mr. Martin says when he doesn't want to forget something, he sets it down beside his chewing tobacco."

"MISS FAWN LIPPINCUT is a clever recitationist and trims her own hats. . . . [She] is the author of "How To Hold Your Husband's Love Through the Rhubarb Season" and she has also sent a number of recipes to the newspapers that show marked literary ability. Miss Lippincut is single and reconciled."

"CONSTABLE NEWT PLUM is one of those rare characters whom nature sometimes raises out of most inhospitable soil. Mr. Plum was born in 1845 on a fertile farm in the Mad River Valley near Pickletown, Ohio. . . . After a course in broom making, he wandered to Brown County, Indiana, where he worked for some years as a field hand, playing pool in the evenings and saving his money. Being of a modest disposition, he hoarded his opinions and soon gained the reputation of being a gentleman of rare ability. After waiting patiently for an off year he was nominated and elected constable, a position he has held for many years. . . ."

"PROFESSOR CLEM HARNER: One very rarely finds a musician possessing the rare ability, both cultivated and native, of Prof. Clem Harner, stowed away in an isolated hamlet. Mr. Harner has made his home in Brown County for fifteen years, and practically nothing is known of his previous life. Since his sweet, silver notes on the cornet first charmed the community, the gossips stopped their speculating and immediately commenced to pay homage to the genius in their midst. He is the organizer and director of the Brown County Silver Cornet Band, which plays on the slightest provocation. . . ."

Kin Hubbard and his friend Will Rogers. *(Lilly Library, Indiana University)*

Kin Hubbard's creation, Abe Martin of Brown County, appeared in more than 300 newspapers daily for years.

"MISS TAWNEY APPLE first attracted public attention with her snappy contributions to various poultry journals, and her many invaluable hints to farmers were eagerly sought after. . . .

"She is the real type of the literary woman, affecting a bulky appearance, caring little or nothing for her hair, and eating raw onions on Sunday. She makes her home with the family of Elgin Tyler, her father and mother having been killed by a corn shredder two years ago. . . ."

"PINKY KERR is a slip-horn player of rare ability and when he is not traveling with some troupe he makes his home with his sister, Mrs. Bunker Hooper. He relates many interesting stories of his travels, of famous managers who have skinned him, of narrow hotel escapes, of having been poisoned on canned corn at Hurley, Wisconsin, and of walking home from Albuquerque, New Mexico."

"TELL BINKLEY: There are thousands of Tell Binkleys. Clean cut, affable fellows, considerate, kindly, and execution proof; taking large interest in public affairs; selling oil land today and mining stock tomorrow; prominent at all gatherings and foremost in group photographs; the head and spirit of all movements for betterment of town and city; borrowing here and there and paying eventually; drinking or leaving it alone; always sympathetic and kind.

"Tell Binkley came to Brown County ten years ago, and he has been expecting a check from somewhere every day since. . . . He is still the same whole-souled, polished, kindly gentleman, liberal to a fault and sharing his massive touring car with the highest and humblest citizen alike. . . ."

"UNCLE NILES THURSTON TURNER was one hundred and three years old last November. . . . He retains his faculties to a wonderful degree, reading the Delphi Journal without the aid of spectacles and remembering when tomatoes were poison and when derby hats were lined like coffins. . . . Mr. Turner claims that he once had a chance to buy the land where Indianapolis now stands for $7.00, but the owner did not have change for a ten. . . . After a perfectly rounded-out career Mr. Turner delights to while away the evening of his life telling the most outrageous and preposterous Indian stories, and scaring little children. He also makes ax handles."

T. C. Steele

Theodore C. Steele came to Brown County just three years after Abe Martin did, building south of Belmont the home he later called "The House of the Singing Winds." His second wife wrote a book by the same name about their experiences here. The house still stands as part of the 211-acre T. C. Steele State Memorial, which can be visited daily, except Monday and major holidays, the year round.

Steele, who was already sixty years old when he moved to Brown County, had become known as an unusually fine, as well as a prolific, portrait painter. Although beginning his painting career as a five-year-old child prodigy near Gosport in Owen County, he had studied art in Chicago, Indianapolis, and at the Royal Academy in Munich, Germany. By the turn of the century, he had already received national and international acclaim, and some said he was the best portrait painter in North America, a claim which has gone undisputed. Among the portraits he painted was one of his good friend, Hoosier poet James Whitcomb Riley.

Landscape painting was strictly a sideline for him, although he did it well. The portraits were his specialty, and he painted many of them. (They also provided a way to make a living, so that he could paint the landscapes.) Sometimes he would do as many as three portraits during a single day after he moved to Brown County. He produced hundreds, even thousands of them.

"Part of the reason he was so prolific," said Bill Weddle, superintendent of the T. C. Steele Memorial and a scholar of Steele as an artist and personality, "is because his second wife, who was twenty-five years younger than he, apparently drove him to it. We've had visitors here who knew Steele personally and some of them have remarked his second wife 'was mean to him.'" When he died in 1926, there were more than 700 paintings in his barn studio at his home. But there were others scattered around the world.

As a young artist, he sold some of his works for just $2 each and it was unusual when he collected $10 for a portrait. He made his money because he was prolific. But as he became better known and more sought after, the works began selling for $2,000 or more. Weddle said some of his works have now sold for as much as $8,000 for a single painting; others for $4,000 each. A number of his paintings are on display at the studio now, and a great many of his drawings, charcoal sketches, some of them made during his studies in Germany, are located at the Steele home, but are not displayed.

Because Steele was an accomplished artist, because he was also prolific and admired by so many artists and had built quite a following before he came to Brown County, it was easy for his move here to attract other artists. And it did. If T. C. Steele had found something in Brown County, then it must be good for others as well. And they came—from Indianapolis and Chicago mostly, and a few from other points. The visiting artists would gather at the old Pittman Hotel, which stood about where McDonald's Chevrolet garage now stands in Nashville, and would travel on foot and by horse and buggy, rented from the livery stable, to the backroads where they could sketch and paint. And they, in turn, sold their works. Every time they did, it was another plus for Brown County.

Steele, meanwhile, although labeled the "father of Brown County's art colony," was never very much a part of it. He was too far away. During horse and buggy days, the House of the Singing Winds south of Belmont was a far piece from Nashville. And there were no accommodations in those parts. So artists seldom got there. They came instead to Nashville via the railroad to Helmsburg, where they were picked up and brought to the Pittman Hotel or to a boarding house. But Steele was

T. C. Steele. *(Lilly Library, Indiana University)*

The House of the Singing Winds, T. C. Steele's home and studio near Belmont.

known, admired, highly respected, and honored by them. He kept a studio gallery in Indianapolis from which he sold many of his paintings. He made frequent trips back there, dividing his time between the capital city and Brown County. And during some winters, he rented a place in Bloomington, where he and his wife lived until the spring returned to the Hills O'Brown.

One of the reasons Steele came to Brown County, of course, was because he possessed a finely honed appreciation of nature. It was an element that raised the level of his art above the ordinary. This communication with nature instilled in him the wisdom and skill that he expressed in his art and made him famous not only on this continent, but other continents as well.

Among those artists who came either about the same time or in the years to follow who were influenced by Steele were portraitist Marie Goth, who established a summer studio in Nashville in 1923, only three years before Steele's death; C. Curry Bohm, Will Vawter, V. J. Cariani, Carl Graf, Anthony Buchta, Dale Bessire, Louis O. Griffith, Ada Walter Shulz and Alberta Shulz, as well as contemporary artists C. Carey Cloud, Kay Pool, and a score of others.

Even before Steele had moved to Brown County, Adolph Shulz came to tour the area by horse and buggy and later described his discovery: "Never before had I been so thrilled by a region; it seemed like a fairyland with its narrow winding roads leading the traveler down into the creek beds, through the water pools and up over the hills."

Many other artists were to follow, some of them homebred. Others moved from other points until today there are more than fifty professional artist-painters in Brown County including the nationally acclaimed wildlife artist Bill Zimmerman, who published a portfolio of prints back in 1974 that sold for $1,000 a copy. Today, they have become collector's items.

Just how far down the line the Steele influence has carried is debatable, of course, and it is apparently waning, but it certainly had an impact in earlier days. If Steele had not come to Belmont, Brown County might never have become an art colony at all, certainly not the art colony it is today.

Frank Hohenberger. *(Lilly Library, Indiana University)*

Frank Hohenberger

Just ten years after T. C. Steele came to live in Brown County, photographer Frank Hohenberger, with a homemade camera and not much else to his name, packed up and moved to Brown County in 1917. He came, he said, because he felt there was something for him here. And there was, for Hohenberger lived the rest of his life among the Hills O'Brown. He was very much a loner, and he never married, but he was dedicated to his photography and to the cause of conservation.

Hohenberger's effect upon the county was quite different from that of T. C. Steele or of Kin Hubbard. His role was one of documentation and he did an extraordinarily fine job of it. The characters portrayed by his camera were here—honest, hardworking people showing the simple but sometimes harsh beauty of their lifestyles. Although he did the people best, Hohenberger was also, just as Steele and Hubbard were, a lover of nature. All three were strict practitioners of conservation.

At one time, Hohenberger went on a campaign to keep the trees of the county from being cut, particularly those along the roadways. He pleaded with farmers not to cut their fencerows, but to leave them for wildlife habitat. A fencerow with trees possesses character, he said, but one that is barren holds little interest for anyone.

Hohenberger was not only a portrait photographer, he was an excellent nature photographer. But most of all, he captured the spirit of Brown County. And that spirit became publicized in numerous periodicals and magazines, including *Good Housekeeping*. The log cabin culture of Brown County became well known through Hohenberger in California, New York, and Florida, indeed across much of America.

In 1933, Hohenberger described Nashville to a magazine writer thus: "When I moved here, this was a place with only about 300 population, with two groceries, a livery stable, a drug store and a boarding house; a village far off the railroad with no industries; dependent on the trade of the hill folks."

And in his diary, he described Nashville as a place with unpaved streets, wood-burning stoves, individual water supplies, and helpful but curious neighbors. To his friends, he said it was a "village nestling in the valley of peace" where he had found the "restfulness that brings inspiration."

Hohenberger was also a writer, although he never became known for that. For thirty-one years, from 1923 until 1954, he wrote a weekly column for the *Indianapolis Star* called "Down in the Hills o' Brown County." He wrote about whatever struck him, from amusing anecdotes about his neighbors and their idiosyncrasies to political, historical, and educational comment on Brown County. He was, in one sense, a Kin Hubbard, James Whitcomb Riley, and T. C. Steele, all focused through a camera lens. And quite frequently, as with Hubbard, the natives of Brown County took issue with him, objecting to his exposure of their lifestyles to the outside world. Some said he was "ruining the county by telling tales about the people." Some even objected to being called natives; they contended instead that was a term to be assigned to Filipinos or people in darkest Africa.

As his diary reflected, Hohenberger possessed a real love and understanding of the people of Brown County, however, and of the land itself. He was, although he often argued the point, a bystander who was not actually a part of the community or the people, but someone who stood aside and interpreted its movement.

His life was always simple, although not as much so as many of the people he portrayed. His needs were few and he spent most of his money on new and better camera equipment, always experimenting with something new. "It would not do," he once said, "to come to Brown County to paint the simple life unless you live it for the time being at least. Folks won't take well to you."

Among some of the entries in his diary were these, reflecting some of the spirit infusing Hohenberger's world.

"Burt Thurman was sent a gallon of sorghum by an admirer from down here. He didn't know the difference, as witness: He wrote the donor to thank him for the fine honey."

"At the Duncan school race it was quite overcast and an outsider wanted to know if the sun ever shone here, and if it did, where in hell did it come up at—he was lost."

"March 6, 1922, Dick Coffey had a funeral over south and it was necessary to take two horses and two mules to pull the hearse. Someone remarked that it must have been a Democrat, for they don't allow them on Republican funerals."

"And there's the story of the children near Gatesville with a family of cats. The children decided they should baptize the cats and immersed all but old Tom. Girl couldn't get him under. Boy said, sprinkle him and let him go to hell."

"Ever since several stills were rounded up here folks don't seem so particular as to who helps them on with their overcoats."

"Mr. Grattan died Friday morning and as he did not wish to be embalmed he was buried the next day after dinner. Some town wag suggested in connection with the hurried plantin' that he had been here long enough anyway."

Commenting on the Stone Head monument, he inscribed: "Leonard Wheeler told me that the stone had fallen into the creek at one time and laid there for 10 years. Wes Polley, a road contractor, came along and dug it out. Hill Coffey of Nashville retraced the lettering and it was placed on a cement pillar. [Name deleted] said to have been drunk, shot the nose from the face."

"[Warden] Oliver said when he went to arrest an old man on David's Branch for hunting on Sunday the fellow said, 'Yes, I know it's agin the law, and besides I used to be a warden under Sweeney of Columbus.' He wanted Oliver to release him, saying: 'Let's forget this and go and have some watermelon.' A little later he [Oliver] caught Jesse Mathis and Louis Selmier, both hunting on Sunday. Jesse said he was never known to do anything wrong but what he got caught at it. When he started for Selmier Oliver had to shoot once to cause a stop. When the two met Oliver asked him why he run, and Louis said he wasn't running—he just couldn't keep his feet still. Then Louis wanted to know what Oliver wanted. The first thing the warden asked for was a chew of tobacco. Then they were both told to come to town, but first get their dinner. Oliver was at the hardware store to greet them and Jesse told Oliver that he had been thinking things over and decided he hadn't been hunting—it was the dog. 'But you done the shooting, didn't you?' inquired Oliver."

During most of his forty-odd years spent in Brown County until his death in 1963, Frank Hohenberger argued the cause of photography as an art form and some of his most bitter arguments were with some of his artist-painter friends. Sometimes he became sarcastic. "There's nothing at all to taking pictures," he said. "Why, it's easy according to artists. Just like a mechanical toy—you wind it up and it does the rest." But later the Brown County Art Gallery Association made him an honorary member "because of his contribution to art through the camera lens." He would have been especially happy to know the Herron Art Museum in Indianapolis in 1967, a few years after his death, held an exhibition of his work. A major collection of his photographs is at the Lilly Library, Indiana University, Bloomington.

The works of Hohenberger were not confined to Brown County, however. Some of his finest character studies were along the tidewater areas of the Carolinas, in Kentucky, and in Mexico. But he spent most of his life here, driving the backroads and searching for new vistas to portray, new faces for character study. Although, like most photographers, he took some bad photographs along with the good, he was unquestionably a master artist and his work becomes more highly acclaimed with each passing year. If he were alive, he would be pleased indeed.

Photographs by Hohenberger. *(Lilly Library, Indiana University)*

Homecoming. *(Lilly Library, Indiana University)*

The Wooded Playground

3

Land of Trees

One of the primary reasons Brown County has remained beautiful is because of its large number of trees. Most of the hills and hollows are clothed in trees and, in fact, most of the county is forested. The principal trees which contribute all that fall color which brings thousands of visitors to the hills of Brown are tulip poplar, sassafras, redbud, dogwood, elm, maple, beech, oak, and hickory.

A land-use study by the U.S. Soil Conservation Service shows that 176,830 acres of the 207,360 acres in the county are forested. There are another 1,470 acres in wetland, plus 2,050 acres covered with water. Approximately 15,930 acres are used for agriculture.

Of those forested acres, Yellowwood State Forest covers some 22,457 acres, most of it wooded; Brown County State Park, largest in the state park system, has 15,543 acres; and the Hoosier National Forest has nearly 17,000 acres in Brown County. Of that area, nearly 8,000 acres would be contained in the projected Salt Creek Wilderness Area.

The Wooded Playground

The Hills O'Brown have long been known for their scenery, but they also provide a great mecca for those seeking out a diverse playground. You can fish, swim, boat, camp, ride horseback, picnic, bicycle, hike, hunt, ski, or canoe in Brown County. With the advent of the ski resorts, the area offers a year-round recreation program.

The greatest attraction, unlike most playgrounds, is not water but the rugged territory and the wooded hills. Hiking and horseback riding offer the greatest spring, summer, and fall activities and, in winter, sledding downhill and cross-country skiing. The combination of vast public lands, interesting rugged trails, beautiful scenery, and a good wildlife population make Brown County attractive to numbers of people.

The Indiana State Planning Services Agency says more than 67,000 acres, the bulk of it in public lands, is available for recreation pursuits in Brown County. Few counties in the state can offer more in any aspect. Public lakes make up nearly a thousand acres of that figure, and the rest is in woodland, meadow, and stream.

Most popular is Brown County State Park, comprising 15,543 acres, making it the largest state park in Indiana. While it's not as large as Yellowwood State Forest, it is more oriented toward outdoor recreation. Hiking, camping, horseback riding, picnicking, and bicycling are all major endeavors there.

The park contains twenty-seven miles of scenic winding roadways, all hard surface and, except for weekends, is usually light on traffic. They provide excellent places for bicycling, although the hills are steep. The park also has a nature center, many wooded natural areas, and more than eight miles of rugged trails. Nature hikes are conducted by the park naturalist twice daily during the summer months and on weekends during the spring and autumn. All of the hiking trails are open during winter for cross-country skiing, provided there are sufficient snow depths (5–6 inches) to prohibit erosion. Nearly a hundred miles of horseback riding trails are also open for skiing during winter. Rental horses are available at the saddle barn in the state park.

Bank fishing is permitted on either of the two lakes—Strahl and Ogle—but a state fishing license is required, of course. Bass and bluegill are the two principal species; spring is considered the best season. Spring is also a good season to hunt for edible mushrooms in the park, and hundreds of people come in search of giant morels as large as any to be found in the lower Midwest.

More than two hundred sites are provided for camping at the state park, many of them with electric hookups. During peak weekends and holidays, however, the campground quickly fills up. A small overflow area is utilized, but after that, campers are turned away.

An Olympic-sized swimming pool with modern service building, which can handle 2500 swimmers, near the north entrance of the park is open Memorial Day to Labor Day. Classes in swimming are conducted periodically. Swimming is not permitted in the lakes.

Much of the recreation activity at Yellowwood State Forest centers around Yellowwood Lake, containing 133 acres and a meandering shoreline surrounded by woodlands and open meadows. But there are also horse and hiking trails, picnic areas, and campgrounds. Rowboats (no motors are permitted) can be rented for use on Yellowwood Lake at the boat dock near the forest headquarters.

Stream canoeing in Brown County is limited, however. Bean Blossom Creek in the area around Trevlac to Lake Lemon is navigable, but is virtually dead paddling. Salt Creek from Nashville to Lake Monroe is navigable, but you may have to drag your canoe over logs or riffles in some places. Best time to canoe is during the spring when streams have more water than during the summer. You can bring your own canoe, or rentals are available from Mike Nickels, Rt.4, Box 172, Nashville, Phone (812) 988-2689.

For those interested in a more organized outdoor recreation program, the Brown County Inn at Nashville offers a complete recreation program with a fulltime recreation director. While the program is primarily for guests, visitors or residents may also join the Recreation Club on an annual basis which permits them use of the indoor heated swimming pool, sauna, tennis courts, and a miniature golf course. Canoes are also available to guests, and they may use them on Salt Creek which flows along the rear of the Inn property.

From Thanksgiving until early March, the recreation trend is toward downhill skiing. Two resorts—Long Mountain and Nashville Alps, located on SR 46 near Nashville at Green Valley and Schooner Valley respectively—offer first-rate accommodations on the slopes. Both resorts employ snow-making equipment to lay down a base on the slopes. Ski instruction is available.

One of the best and most inexpensive ways of experiencing Brown County is by hiking. You can do it virtually year round, although the spring months of April and May and the fall months of September, October, and November are best. A whole complex of trails extending throughout the county are available and are well maintained. That includes the Ten O'Clock Line Trail, Tulip Tree Trace, and Yellowwood Trail, which together cover a good portion of the county.

In addition, there are trails in the Yellowwood State Forest and in Brown County State Park as well as the Hickory Ridge Hiking Trail in the Hoosier National Forest around the upper end of Lake Monroe. This trail alone is twenty miles in length and covers some of the most scenic, hilly, and forested areas Indiana has to offer. More than 360 species of wildlife are found in this area, including wild turkey, bobcat, bald eagle, and deer.

Maps and brochures on the Hickory Ridge Hiking Trail are available from the Hoosier National Forest, U.S. Forest Service, Bedford, IN 47421. A map covering all major trails in the county is available for a small fee from Lee Nading, PO Box 1805, Bloomington, IN 47402.

Trail Headquarters, a non-profit outdoor education organization located atop Bear Wallow Hill at Flags of the Nations, sponsors several challenging hiking and bicycling trails in the area. These include Flags of the Nations Trail, Yellowwood Trail, Ten O'Clock Line Trail, Tulip Tree Trace, and Flags of the Nation Trail. Lengths of these trails range from 12 to 26 miles. Campsites are provided near the trail heads or ends. Awards are given to those who hike the trails. Additional information is available by contacting Trail Headquarters, Route 4, Bear Wallow Hill, Nashville, IN 47448. Or just follow the Flags of the Nation signs on Greasy Creek Road, which leads off old SR 46 on the eastern edge of Nashville.

Some of the best lake fishing in Brown County is available at Lake Monroe (the upper end) and at Yellowwood Lake. Some five- and six-pound largemouth bass have been taken in both places. Crooked Creek Lake, also located on Yellowwood State Forest lands, is considerably smaller, but has provided good fishing in the past. Any size boat may be used on Lake Monroe, and there's a launching ramp at Crooked Creek, south of Belmont. Only rowboats and canoes may be used on Crooked Creek Lake. Channel catfish are also available in Yellowwood Lake, and trout (brown and rainbow) are stocked annually in Jackson Creek, just above the Lake.

The portion of Lake Monroe in Brown County is also an excellent place for stillwater canoeing and shallow draft boats. Much of the area is very shallow and an excellent place for bird-watching and wildlife studies via boat or canoe. Mallard ducks and some other types of waterfowl nest in this area, and great wading birds such as great blue heron are quite often seen in this area. Sometimes bald eagles are spotted here, usually during late fall or mild winters.

You may enjoy primitive camping at Crooked Creek ramp free of charge. Primitive camping is also available at Yellowwood Lake.

Private camping with full hookups and modern facilities is available at KOA just east of Nashville on SR 46 during the spring, summer, and fall months.

Additional information may be gained on all aspects of outdoor recreation in Brown County by writing the Chamber of Commerce, Nashville, IN 47448.

The Yellowwood Tree

Although the Yellowwood State Forest in Brown County, covering some 22,500 acres, was named after the rare yellowwood tree, the largest number of them are found not in the state forest, but in Ogle Hollow Nature Preserve in Brown County State Park. In fact, sixty-three of the trees known to exist in all of Indiana are in Ogle Hollow. Others are located elsewhere in the park and in Yellowwood State Forest.

The 41-acre tract faces north, bordering steep ravines and a secluded valley. And it was here in 1933 the first yellowwood trees were discovered. While they're more plentiful in the Carolinas, Tennessee, and Kentucky, the yellowwood is considered a most rare tree in Indiana. If you should visit there, look for a smooth gray bark similar to the common American beech. Yellowwood bark, while similar to beech, is often spotted with green lichens, has a softer texture and is subject to frost cracks. The wood is a bright yellow color and yields a yellow dye.

The leaf is about two times larger than the beech leaf, however, measuring 10 to 12 inches in length. The tree is medium-sized, attaining a height of about 50 feet. It also produces legume seed pods 2 to 3 inches long. Flowers are showy white panicles drooping from the ends of brittle branches.

The nature trail leading through Ogle Hollow offers a good look at yellowwood trees, and the brochure, available at the Nature Center, will help you to identify them.

Birch Monroe hugs a young fan at the Bluegrass Festival.
(Barbara Sheehan)

A group of musicians practice at Bill Monroe's Bluegrass Festival.
(Barbara Sheehan)

Bill Monroe. *(Barbara Sheehan)*

An informal group at the Bluegrass Festival. *(Barbara Sheehan)*

Performers on stage at Bill Monroe's Bluegrass Festival, Bean Blossom. *(Barbara Sheehan)*

Artist Louise Kissling paints the house of her neighbor, Emmy Moore, on the Bellsville-Mt. Liberty Road.

Those Other Artists

4

Carey Cloud

Brown County artist C. Carey Cloud came to Brown County in the 1940s. He was then known as "the man from Whistleville." Cloud for 24 years designed the toys found in boxes of Crackerjack. Known locally now as the Andrew Wyeth of Brown County, Cloud figures that if children played only six minutes each with his toys, he provided about 4,000,000-play hours for children across America each year. He retired from toy designing in 1964.

Those Other Artists

Crafts were a part of the Brown County scene long before there were artists painting pictures here. And the ranks of craftsmen have increased year by year until it would seem there's room for no more in the Hills O'Brown.

Handicrafts were an integral part of the lives of the early settlers here. They wove baskets, spun yarn threads to make cloth, quilted their own bedcovers, sewed their own clothes, and in later years, did woodcarving for the few tourists that came their way. The crafts were simple, but varied.

One thing that makes Brown County unique, however, is the fact that many of those early-day crafts have been kept alive over the years. There still is candlestick making, basket weaving, homemade soap, spinning and weaving and carding of wool. Metal sculpture has become a big thing. Many of the little shops on South Van Buren Street and at other places in Nashville reflect the wares and crafts of local cabin industries. Jim Stamper and his wife, Judy, create fine quality miniature furniture so intricate they must work with a magnifying glass. Donn Stoffer, a leading metal sculptor, specializes in water fountains and has created more than 1,600 of them sold in many parts of the nation. A 7.5-ton Stoffer creation decorates the lobby of the Marriott Hotel in Clarksville, Indiana, across the Ohio River from Louisville.

John Mills, the potter, keeps busy most of the year turning out fine pottery (about 5,000 pieces each year) for visitors to take home with them. Most of the stoneware he makes is bought as a souvenir, a reminder of one's visit to Brown County. John still uses an old foot-powered potter's wheel in his tiny shop in back of the Old Ferguson House of Antiques.

The variety of products produced by craftsmen in Brown County today is phenomenal. There are almost as many products as there are craftsmen—and there seem to be hundreds of the latter. Many of them work out of their homes in the backwoods; others work in shops in Nashville or Bean Blossom or other towns. Some do stained glass creations, leatherwork, weaving, crocheting, quilting, glass-blowing, knitting, candle-making. Others do dried weed and flower arrangements. The list is nearly endless, and each year there seem to be some new ideas, some new craft in the county.

In the late 1970s, the Crafts Guild was founded by Susan Showalter, who does leatherwork and quilting, in an effort to create a greater awareness of the variety of crafts available in Brown. In 1980, there were about 60 members of the guild, and about 36 members of the Crafts Guild Gallery, which markets the wares of local crafts persons. The gallery is located upstairs over Long John Silvers Restaurant on South Van Buren Street.

Jack Brubaker, blacksmith, who is also a member of the guild, says the gallery gives the crafts people an opportunity to sell their wares and at the same time be working away from the crowds in their own shops. Jack welcomes visitors, but wants only those who are genuinely interested in blacksmithing.

"I used to have my shop in Nashville," he said, "and I found it much more difficult to work. Now I work out here in the country (his shop is on SR 135 south just north of Van Buren School), and there are few interruptions." Jack uses an old-type forge and makes just about anything anyone wants him to make. "My customers come to me because they've heard of my work, tell me what they want, and together we draw up some rough plans and go from there. It can be anything from a custom-built wood stove to a candlestick," he said.

Jack Brubaker working in his blacksmith shop. His wares are sold through the Crafts Gallery in Nashville.

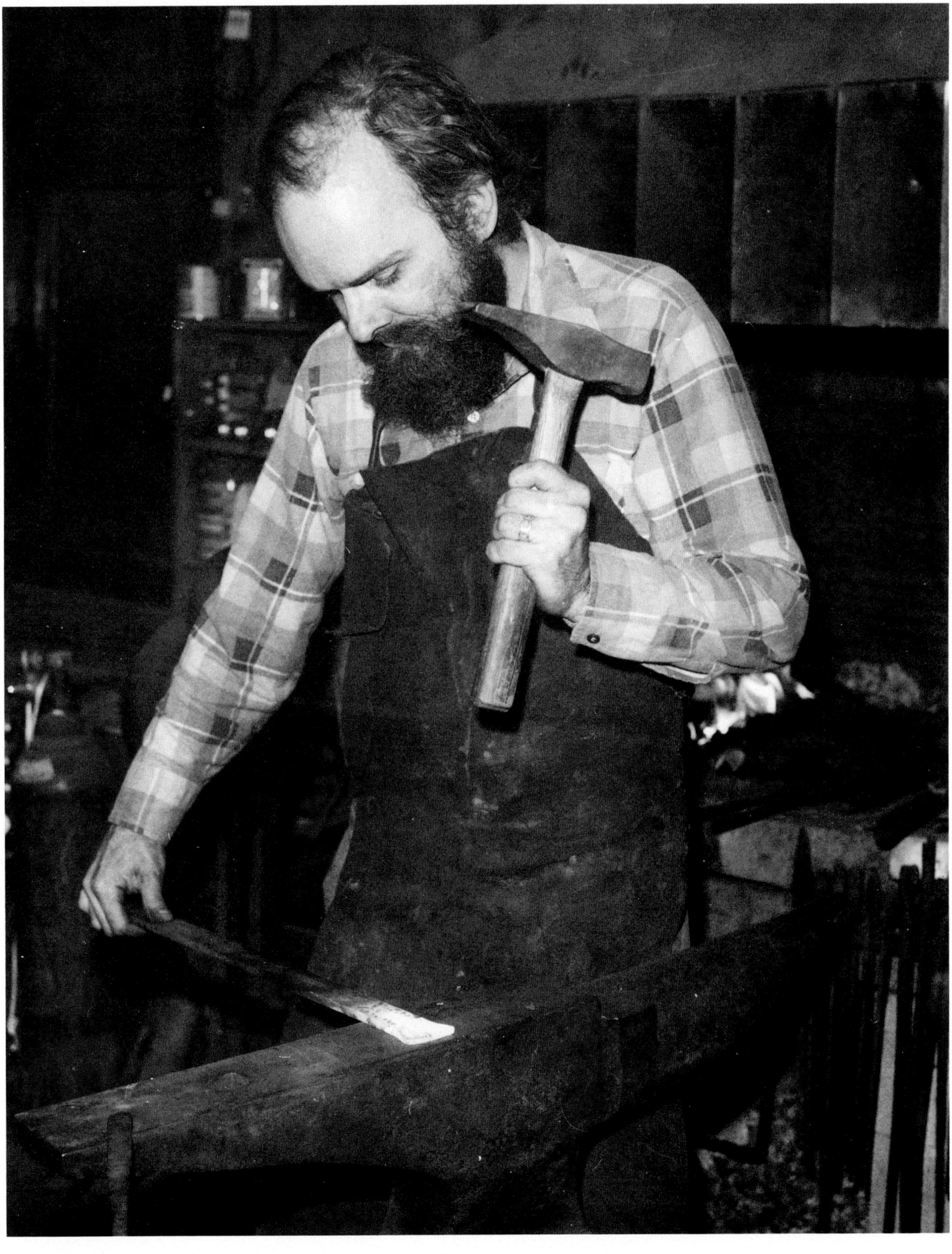

Jess Allen uses a froe to split white oak logs into basket splits.

Turning Back the Clock

A few Brown County families have, in essence, turned back the clock in their lifestyles. Jess and Twilla Allen of Old Helmsburg Road live without benefit of electricity or running water. Their house in the woods will be, when completed, a study in self-sufficiency. They raise goats for milk and chickens for meat and eggs, and use wood for heat. They make baskets and do stained-glass artwork to bring the income needed for buying groceries.

Jess says he would guess there are a dozen or so families in Brown County who have decided to live without modern conveniences, among them Jack Brubaker, a blacksmith, and his wife. "We find life much simpler and less susceptible to inflation," said Allen. The Allens are well educated, as are some of the other couples. They decided to go this route just to simplify their lives and get back to the basics.

The Allens' basket work can be seen at the Brown County Craft Guild's gallery above Long John Silvers in Nashville.

Jack Brubaker, of course, is a full-time professional craftsman. Others, like Pat Richardson, who lives east of Bean Blossom and makes cutie dolls from panty hose and used clothing picked up at garage sales, or Mrs. Mary Richhart of Spearsville, who is 79 and among the most talented quilters in the entire Midwest, do it strictly as a sideline. But they are all a part of the crafts picture in the Hills O'Brown.

Donn Stoffer, who has been around Brown County practically all his life and is a former member of the Brown County Chamber of Commerce board of directors, finds it unbelievable. "There are a lot of crafts," he said, "many of them very fine ones. And then there's junk, too. But if there weren't the junky things, then people wouldn't really come to appreciate the finer crafts. One lends perspective to the other."

While Stoffer sells a lot of his creations in The Trilogy in Nashville, he keeps his shop at Stone Head, out in the county. "I can work out here," he said, "away from the maddening crowds." Before he moved into the old store building at Stone Head, he had his shop at New Bellsville.

Even though there are large numbers of craftsmen in the county, they seem to fare better in many ways than do the artists. For the tourists tend to buy more crafts than they do paintings or works of art from the artists. The Chamber of Commerce doubts there are more than two dozen full-time professional artists in Brown County who make their entire livelihood from the work. The crafts fare a bit better than that.

Of course, some craftsmen also consider themselves artists, so it's a line of considerable debate, and perhaps there is no definitive answer. Metal sculpture, most would agree, certainly is art. But so is working with stained glass. So perhaps the line between the two is very thin indeed.

As John Mills once said: "There's a little bit of art to everything."

William Lee of Schooner Valley makes violins, called fiddles by most Brown Countians, at his home. He is also an excellent fiddle player.

Pat Richardson's Groucho Marx doll, made from pantyhose and garage sale clothes.

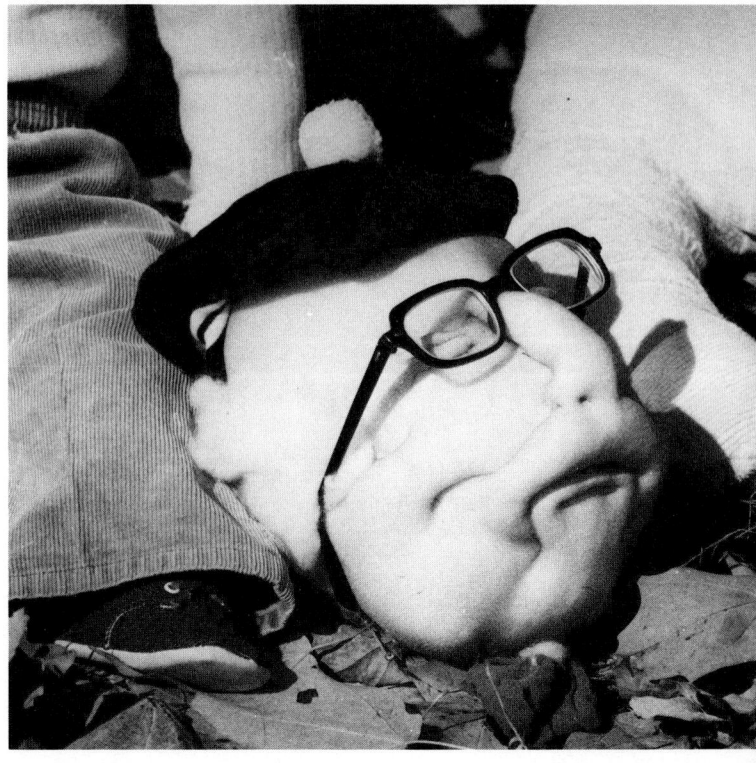

Jim Stamper and his wife, Judy, fashion miniature furniture at their home and sell the pieces through Brown County shops.

Barbara Bowen is one of several women in Brown County who still takes spinning seriously. (*Barbara Sheehan*)

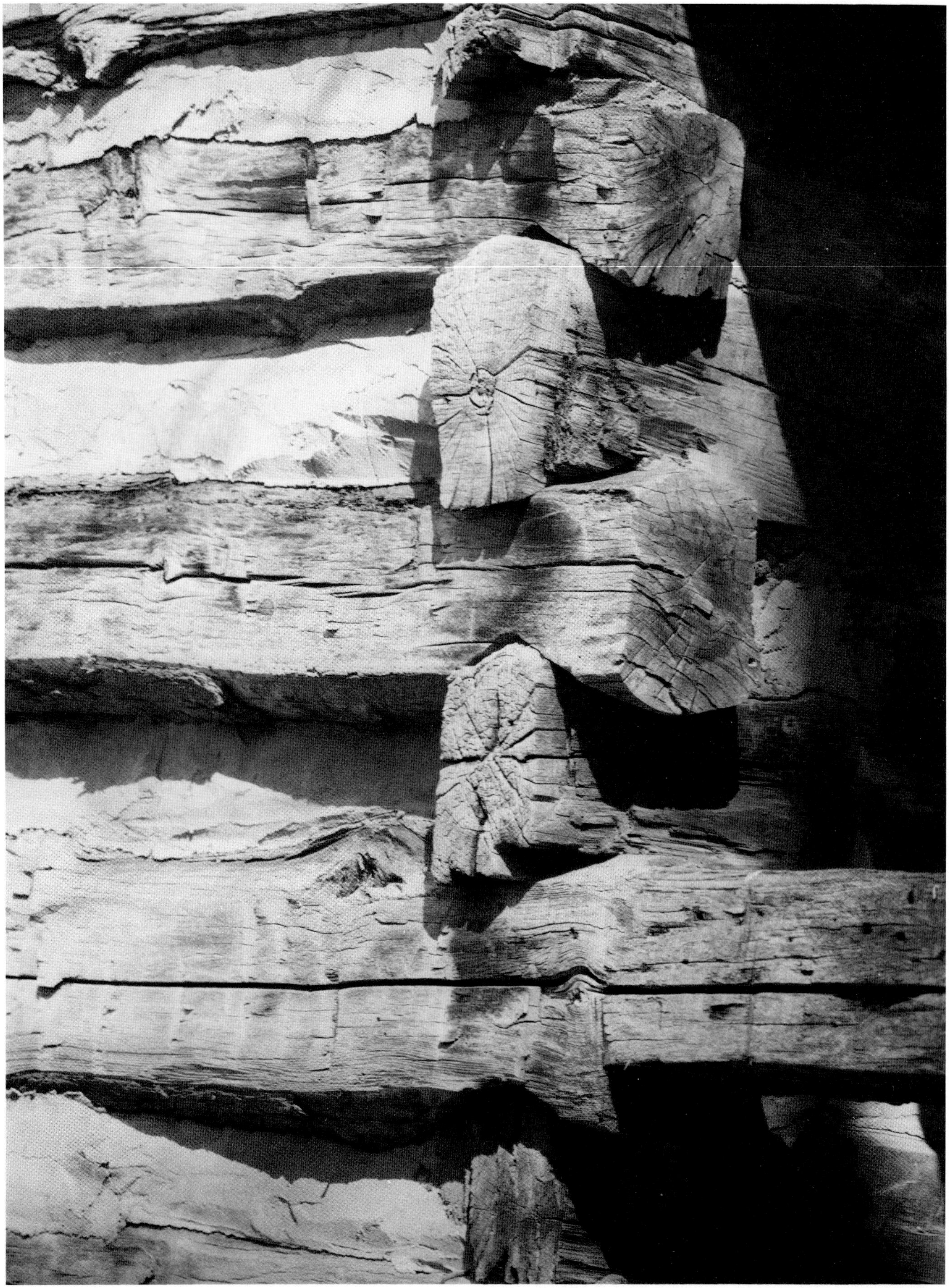

People & Lifestyles

5

Little Orphant Annie

Remember that remarkable poem created by Hoosier poet James Whitcomb Riley, called "Little Orphant Annie"? In Riley's book, *Child Rhymes,* published in 1920, it was the lead poem, and accompanying it was a drawing by Brown County artist Will Vawter of "Little Orphant Annie." Well, that "Little Orphant Annie" is also one of Brown County's own dear children, little Sarah Spicer, who was just nine years old then. She's a mite older now, but she still remembers vividly posing for the artist Will Vawter when he sketched the illustrations used in Riley's book.

Sarah Spicer is now Mrs. Sarah Harden of Nashville and has 12 children and 50 grandchildren of her own. Until 1979, she was the school crossing guard near the Nashville IGA on South Van Buren.

Not only was Sarah Spicer the model for "Little Orphant Annie," but also for several other sketches in the book, including one entitled "The Happy Little Cripple" and another called "The Sudden Shower." Her brother was also in some of the drawings.

Log Cabin Country

When the first settlers moved into Brown County in the 1820s, one of their first tasks was to carve out of the woodlands shelter for themselves. They did it with the log cabin. Ever since, the log cabin has been somewhat symbolic of Brown County, and up to half a dozen new cabins, or houses, are being constructed each year. They are a part of the rustic atmosphere prevailing here.

Unquestionably, there are more log cabins in Brown County than in any other county in the state, perhaps the nation. It has become, through tradition, a veritable land of log cabins. At least three companies are involved in their construction. And all of them are keeping busy.

The Brown County Chamber of Commerce, which promotes do-it-yourself tours through log cabin country each spring, estimates there are between 350 and 450 log cabins, or houses, in the county and the number is growing. Some are multistoried, but the majority are one-level houses with possibly an attic on the second floor. Most are simple, both in design and character, but Mike Nickels, who spends virtually all of his time in the construction of log cabins, says they make good sense in today's energy-conscious world. They represent, he thinks, a return to the basics of life. He says they are easy to maintain, easy to heat, and easy to cool during the summer. And if built right, they can be very attractive as well, he added.

Nickels, who says he averages building from three to five log cabin structures each year, normally uses old logs. He locates log houses in other parts of the country, sometimes traveling throughout parts of Indiana, Illinois, and Kentucky seeking out old logs he can buy and transport to Brown County. Once purchased, the building must be carefully razed, making sure that each log is numbered and labeled so it can be reconstructed just the same way.

"After a building has lived a few years, the logs begin to settle into a certain form, the notches mold together, and they would be ill fitted if removed to another position," Nickels said. "So we try to put them back just the way they were in the original structure."

The Brown County Community Building in Nashville is one of the largest log structures in the county.

Not all new log homes are reconstructed, however. Some logs come from a prefabricated kit shipped in and built on the spot with all new logs. Others are sawmill logs slabbed out at a local mill. Nickels is wary of the latter. "These could cause problems in the future," he said, "for they usually aren't seasoned out. They'll warp and split and shrivel up, and the chinking may then fall out from between the logs. Some of these logs we're using in reconstruction might have taken six or seven years to season, so they were completely dried out before being used. That's a long time, but it's necessary to get good construction."

Nickels believes in what he's doing. "The reason I stay with it," he said, "is because I feel like I'm taking something that someone put a lot of time and effort into a lot of years ago and renewing it, preserving it . . . to me, that's a fascinating prospect."

While building a log house in any form takes a lot of pure "grunt" work, Nickels claims it really isn't that difficult. Most of the big long, heavy logs go above the windows and doors and usually there are no more than three or four of them to be lifted. "We do most of our hoisting by muscle power, but occasionally we have to use a hoist to get them raised into place. In the old days, of course, the settlers had house-raisings, and men and women came from miles around to help out. There was always plenty of manpower."

During the old days, of course, the logs were hewn out with a broadax and an adz, which took a lot of time. But labor was cheap, and time was more plentiful. Most log houses were made of poplar, which was soft and easy to work with; Nickels finds some of his old log homes come in oak, however, a much heavier wood with which to deal.

Cost of a log structure home is no savings today. In fact, it's comparable to any other type of construction, ranging about $45 per square foot (in 1980) with promises of healthy increases.

Best time for traveling around the Brown County hills looking at log cabins, of course, is during the winter or early spring. Then you can see the house more plainly because of the lack of foliage. In summer, it's sometimes difficult to see a house even at 100 feet distance. The annual spring log cabin tour features open house at several log cabins in the county, giving visitors an opportunity to get a close-hand look at what it's like to live in one and to meet some of the people who do.

Treasures in Hills O'Brown

The gold rush was never felt in the history of Brown County, but that doesn't mean the precious yellow stuff isn't here. It's not in sufficient quantities to create great wealth—probably never would be—but the chances are good that anyone looking for gold in the little streams of Brown County's glaciated area can find it any day of the year. And not only gold, but diamonds, garnets, rubies, and other precious stones.

Most of the gold prospecting occurred along the North Fork of Salt Creek or along the upper reaches of Bean Blossom Creek and Indian Creek. In fact, at one time commercial gold digging operations were underway, two of them lasting for fifty years. But no one ever claimed they got rich off it.

The gold and precious stones, of course, are souvenirs of the great Ice Age, when much of Indiana was covered with ice. The ice was estimated to be 500 to 600 feet deep at Indianapolis, but south of the city, it began to divide. Parts of it traveled southeast of Brown County, parts of it west. And the thinning portion in between only made it as far as Bean Blossom Creek.

One geologist who did considerable work in this field earlier in this century said if an observer could have stood on one of the hills in Brown County at that time, he would have seen to the east of him a great wall of ice front extending south toward Kentucky, while toward the west it would have been seen in the distance stretching away toward the southwest. For hundreds of miles to the east and west and for 2,000 miles or more to the north, the glaring white desert of snow-covered ice, like that of the interior of Greenland, would have stretched away to the horizon and beyond.

As the glacier melted, however, a terminal moraine was formed, and that's where the gold was left. Almost always found in gold producing areas of the county is black sand which contains black magnetic iron. So whenever you're looking for gold, it might be well to look for black sand first. It's a telltale sign. Although gold is not found always with black sand, gold is seldom found in Brown County without the presence of black sand.

Herman Dine, who lives on Gold Point Road, just south of Peoga, in the northeastern section of the county, is probably the area's best authority on gold prospecting. Now past sixty-five years of age and retired from his job in Indianapolis, Herman returned to the place where he grew up on the banks of Salt Creek. But he and his brother, Morris, have prospected for gold as a hobby ever since they were children. And his sister, Mary Richhart, who now lives near Spearsville, remembers when the Dine family bought all their groceries and whatever clothes they needed from the store with gold. We never used anything else, she recalled.

Herman can still reduce a pan of heavy gravel to gold-bearing sand in about three minutes on Salt Creek, which flows through his front yard. And most of the gold the Dines have found through the years has been on Salt Creek near the junction of Green and Gold Point roads.

"I've got a good collection of gold dust that came out of Salt Creek," said Herman. "And just about everybody who comes here has gone away with gold. If they learn how to do it properly, they're going to find gold. I wouldn't say there are any fortunes to be made, but any serious hobbyist is going to be happy." Dine went on to say he had found some nuggets in the creek, but they are rare. Most of his finds have been flecks of gold dust.

"My greatest find," grinned Dine, "was when I was about seven years old. I remember it well . . . a nugget that weighed 2½ ounces. But gold was so common to us, that I just picked it up and put it in my pocket. All the rest of the day I played around the yard and along the creek, wallowing and rolling on the ground with my dog as a boy of seven will do. That night at supper, I remembered finding the nugget, searched around in my pocket and found it among a few other things I'd picked up during the day. When I plinked it down in front of my father's plate, I thought he was going to choke on the coffee he was drinking. He chugged it down, grabbed his shovel and the gold pan and headed for the spot where I found it before I could finish eating."

During the past few years, Dine has been, as he put it, "pestered to death" by amateur prospectors who have discovered him and his place on Gold Point Road. One fellow from the northern part of the state came with a power loader and before Dine encouraged him to leave had taken about $80 worth of gold out of the creek during one afternoon.

During the early part of this century, gold was dredged from Salt Creek commercially with heavy machinery. Dine worked for that outfit and remembers it well. About $10,000 worth of gold was taken from that operation before it was abandoned during the height of the Great Depression. At today's prices, the gold mined in that operation would have brought more than a quarter million dollars.

One commercial operation actually got underway in Brown County about 1924 when Harrison V. Pittman, a retired Army major, began dredging with a shaker machine powered by a Model T Ford engine. The operation sustained itself, but reported no glowing success. Then in 1932, the Succor Flour Co. financed the purchase of a gold machine—a 48-ton monster with a cubic yard dragline made in Indianapolis by the Engineering Metal Products Company. Cost was $28,000. The Dines worked with the engineer, Gene Williams of Kansas City, about three years on that operation.

Gold prospecting was a vital activity in Brown County long before the turn of the century, however. Before the Civil War, gold prospectors already were panning the streams of Brown County with considerable success. And in 1875 the Brown County Mining Company, incorporated with 2,000 shareholders, began operations in earnest in the search for precious metals and stones. And in 1898 the Indiana Gold Mining and Investment Company, with $100,000 of shareholder capital, was formed. Silver and gold and diamonds, garnets, opals, and sapphires were all found. Best producers were the headwaters of Bean Blossom Creek, the North Fork of Salt Creek, and Indian Creek. The coarsest gold in Brown County was reported in Gosport Hollow Creek, a tributary of Bear Creek.

Herman Dine pans for gold in Salt Creek.

Uncle John Merriman, who lived near Lick Creek, panned for gold for nearly 50 years, 20 of those full-time. The largest nugget he reported taking was found on Bear Creek and weighed 132 grains. On at least two different occasions, Uncle John kept an account of month's labors, Sundays excluded. One month yielded him $34; the other, $40. At today's prices, he would have earned more than $1,000 per month, not considering the valuable stones he found.

Herman Dine thinks there are as many diamonds to be found as there is gold. In fact, at one time the engineer of the company he worked for placed a grease rack under the shaker to catch the tailings. Then they'd melt the hog's lard over a fire, drain it off and count the diamonds. "There were a lot of them," he said. "They were small, but there were a lot of them."

The most precious diamond reported in the county was found during the early part of this century by W. W. Young of near Spearsville who sold it for $200. W. S. Blatchley, the Indiana state geologist from 1894 to 1911, once visited Young and was shown a report from the U.S. Mint at Philadelphia, dated July 1901, showing the mint had received from him 14.05 ounces of gold, which on today's market would be worth nearly $10,000. Young reported he had panned the gold over a period of nine months, but had worked at it only about half time.

According to Blatchley, the quality of gold found in Indiana is considerably superior to that found in California or even in the Klondike. Brown County gold will average 22 or more carats, as against 16 to 18 for California and 14 to 16 for the Klondike.

The gold rush hasn't begun in Brown County yet—probably never will—but that old adage "Thar's Gold in Them Thar Hills" certainly applies to the Hills O'Brown.

How to Pan for Gold

Panning for gold takes stamina and good common sense. As you do more and more of it, the better you'll get. But no prior training is necessary. All you need is a shovel and a gold pan and a pair of knee boots to keep your feet dry, especially if you're planning to do it year round. Your total expenditure should be less than $20 to $25.

If you're only in the shovel and pan stage, you'll find a lot of cooperative landowners along the creeks who won't mind you panning for gold. In fact, people like Herman Dine enjoy helping you, and they'll offer tips on the best places to find it. Use good manners, ask permission before entering one's property, and you'll likely be met with a welcome. In some cases, such as along one stretch of Gold Point Road, the creek runs parallel to the roadway and is open to the public.

Look for black sand along the stream, usually best found in a bend in the stream. Dig up a heaping panful of it, dip your pan down into the water and slough off the coarse rock and mud.

Hold your pan just under the flow of the water, letting it carry away the excess as you swirl the pan and tilt it back and forth. The lighter materials will be carried away by the water. The heavier ones remain. You can toss out the stones with your hand, but soon you'll be down to a handful of black sand on the bottom of the pan. In this, often obscured until you move it around with your fingertips very gingerly, are flecks of gold. And there may also be stones such as garnets, opals, even diamonds. Watch for them. Then pick them out carefully and put them in a jar or some other container you've brought along. A plastic bag is fine as long as it's tough and won't tear.

What could be more discouraging than to find a good-sized nugget and an ounce of flecks and then, at the end of the day, discover the plastic bag has developed a hole through which your cache disappeared.

Gold Pans

Two basic types of gold pans are used by modern-day gold seekers. One is the aluminum pan, the other plastic. Both work well and sell from $3 to $5 each. Available at The Nature House on SR 135 north of Nashville, and The Brown County Rock Shop on Calvin Place in Nashville, both of which have nice collections of Brown County native rocks on sale.

Water Witching

One of the most capable water witches in Brown County is Helen Ayers of Van Buren Township, who works with her husband, a well driller. Helen, unlike many water witchers, uses a dogwood forked stick. Most others use either peach or willow. She has almost a 100 percent batting average.

The water witch, in an area where underground water supplies are scarce except for the bottomlands, is invaluable. The person doing the witching holds to two forked ends of the stick hands up and thumbs out and walks slowly over the ground. When it is over water the point of the stick will turn down. If water is on the surface, as in a creek, the method will not work.

Coat hangers are used by some people to find underground water, or cavities in the earth. In fact, during the Vietnam War, the Marine Corps at Camp Pendleton, California, was training marines to use divining rods to detect tunnels, mines, and booby traps.

Helen, a reporter for *The Brown County Democrat,* says she can also find gas wells, even pipelines and septic tanks, by using the forked dogwood stick.

Natural Walking Canes

George Stephens, whose log cabin nestles in a hollow near the state park boundary north of Elkinsville, lets Mother Nature make unique walking canes for himself and his friends. George helps Mother out by wrapping an old discarded piece of stout electrical cord (rubber coated is best) around and around a small water beech or ironwood bush.

George anchors both ends of the cord tightly so it won't stretch much, then waits patiently the four to six years needed. He then removes the cord and cuts the bush, trimming it at both ends. Lo and behold, the cane looks like a serpent has been wrapped around it. In fact, some people call them serpent canes. The bark can then be peeled, the cane dried, and varnish and shellac applied, if desired. Or you can leave it rustic just the way it was cut in the woods.

Mary Richhart of near Spearsville, standing beside one of her creations, is one of Brown County's oldest and most accomplished quilters.

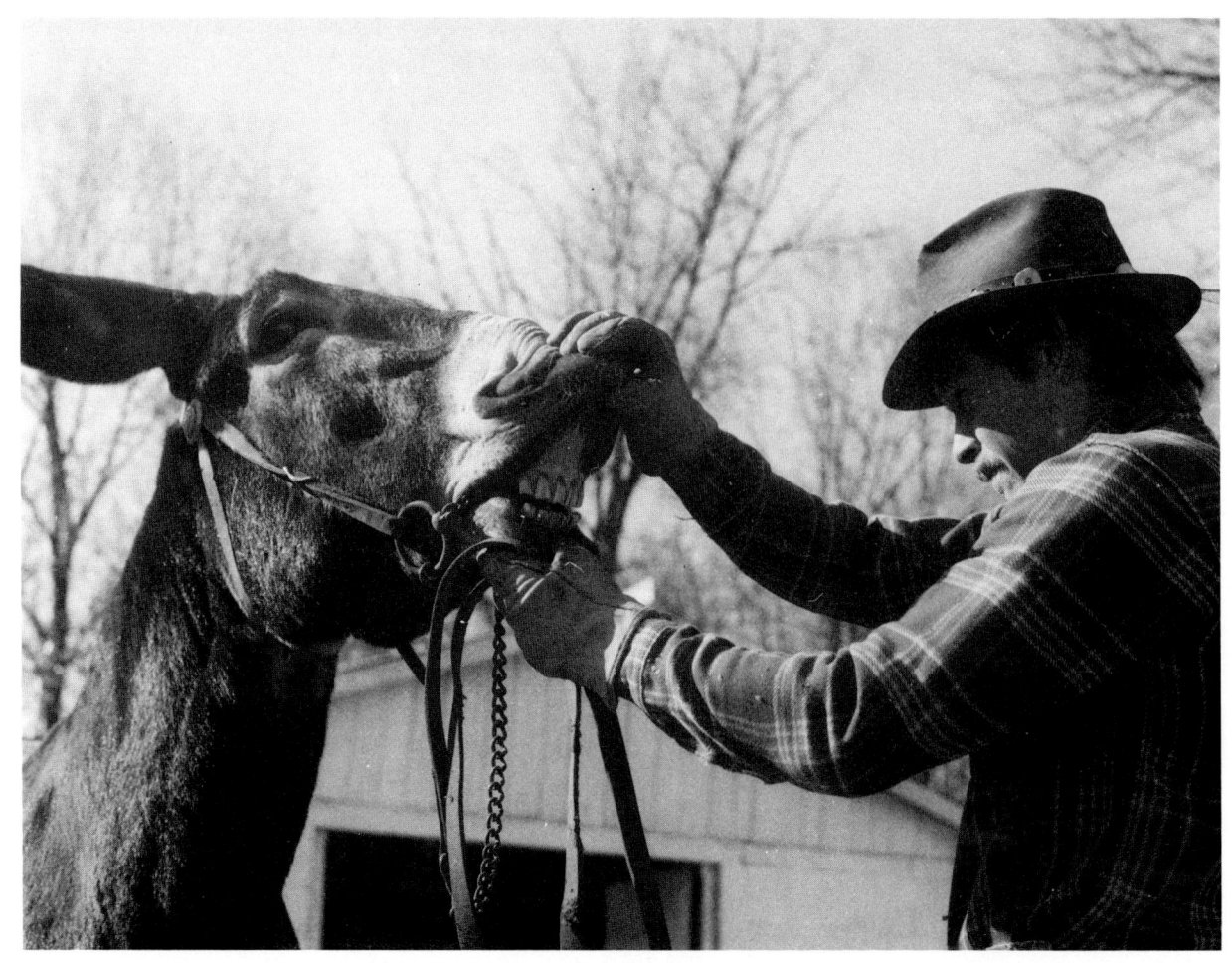

Mule trader Teddy Flynn of Schooner Valley demonstrates how to tell the age of a horse or mule. "Just look the critter right in the mouth," he says.

Shearing sheep at the Poole farm near Spurnica.

Emmy Moore at her home in southeastern Brown County and her "easy" washer.

74

Folklore, Legends, & Other Stuff

Jack, the Wonder Dog

6 It was on a gloomy March day when spring was playing tiddlywinks with winter across Brown County's ridges when I met Jack, the wonder dog. On a backcountry gravel road near Elkinsville, I passed a white frame house and immediately was joined by a huge black dog who ran alongside my car. Of course, I'd had my car chased by dogs all over Brown County, but an eighth of a mile later even at 35 miles an hour, this big black dog was still running either alongside or in front of my car, looking back.

This kept up, and pretty soon I decided Jack wasn't chasing my car; he was running a race with it. I speeded up, and Jack moved to the side of the road. I speeded up more, and out of the corner of my eye, I could see him really stretching out alongside. About the time we hit 50, Jack's tongue began to hang out. And then, as he was looking at me, running silently along without the slightest growl or bark, he stumbled into a hole, and went flip-flop end over end, landing in the ditch. I slowed down, but Jack immediately was back in the race. And about that time, I had run out of road. It dead-ended at the Elkinsville cemetery, which was where I was headed in the first place.

When I got out of the car, Jack came up and grinned at me. And I grinned back, spoke a few words to him, and went about my business of studying gravestones. Jack tired of waiting and left.

An hour later as I was leaving the same route I had come, I passed Jack's house again; he was waiting to join in the race once more. Down the road we went, hooked a sharp left, and climbed over Lucas Hill toward Story. The hill, one of the steepest grade hills in those parts, is gravel, but Jack was way ahead of me looking back at my struggling little car, as though to tell me: "Get on up here . . . give me a challenging run."

When we got to the top of the hill, the terrain leveled out a spell, and I was almost able to catch up to Jack, who by this time was just getting his second wind, and settling down for the long stretch. Down the hill we went, skidded around the sharp bend at the bottom and up the broad Salt Creek floodplain. The road surface was better now, and I was able for a little bit to get the car up to 40 miles an hour. Jack was still ahead of me and stayed there almost to the Salt Creek bridge. I had to slow down to make the bridge, and Jack ran ahead, looking back to see if I was coming.

"This dog ought to be in the Kentucky Derby," I told myself. "Probably outrun any nag they got."

As I headed back up the hard-surfaced straightaway toward Story, I figured I'd better do something to get Jack out of the race. If I didn't, he'd still be running when I got to Gnawbone. I floored the pedal and watched as the speedometer jumped to nearly 70. In my rearview mirror I could still see Jack back the way, leveling out, touching the ground about every eight feet. His tongue was long now, and momentarily I worried he might get a splinter in it, or pick up gravel. Soon I had left him from sight, and apparently, he became discouraged before reaching Story. I never saw him again that day.

75

A few days later, I was back at Elkinsville and decided to stop in at Jack's house. I learned his keeper was Sandy Brown, a nurse in Columbus. Sandy told me she had been given Jack by some friends in Columbus, that he was just past two years old, and she didn't even know the breed. "I just call him a running dog," she said. "He just loves to run . . . would rather run than eat." I could vouch for that.

I was busy on other projects in the northeastern United States and in Florida during the subsequent months, but when I returned in the fall, I again talked to Sandy Brown to learn how Jack was.

"Jack," she said, "hasn't been around in a month. We think he just ran away."

Wherever Jack is, we would bet one thing . . . that he's running, and enjoying every minute of it. Fact is, somebody might have picked him up to enter in the races. Come Derby time, I'm going to be watching closely to see if among the steeds breaking from the starting gate there's a big black dog leveling out for the stretch. If Jack were there, he'd surely be a part of the race—and he might just win it. If he did, he'd have at least two spectators betting on him—Sandy Brown and me.

The Story of the Stone Deer

On a remote hillside in the Brown County State Park is one of the strangest monuments of all—a memorial to the last native deer killed in the area back before the turn of the century. It has become known as the stone deer.

Engraved plainly in the rock is the unmistakable imprint of a magnificent buck deer and above it the mark of a bullet. The man who took it is Rapp H. Pane, whose name is also carved in the rock.

It's an unusual story—this one of the stone deer. It seems Rapp Pane was dependent upon the woodland for the meat that went on his table. He had long since given up hunting deer, for there were no more to be found. Bear had disappeared, too. But there were lots of squirrels, and Rapp Pane spent a lot of time in the woods hunting squirrel. It was on a morning in the autumn of 1897 that he sat silently in the woods watching for squirrel to appear in the trees above him when he spotted, ambling through the woods, this magnificent buck. At first he could not believe his eyes, for no deer had been seen in the area for several years. He sat dumbfounded and somewhat bewildered. He did not want to take its life, but then thoughts flashed before him of the oncoming winter, of his family in need of food. He sat quietly, and the deer still did not notice him. Finally it drew closer, and unable to restrain his urge as a hunter, he raised his gun slowly to his shoulder and fired. The big buck crumpled in its tracks.

Rapp was both glad and sorry, and after slitting the animal's throat to allow the blood to drain upon the ground, he returned to the rock where he sat to contemplate what he had done. It was then he decided to carve a simple monument to the big buck and what apparently was the last deer killed in Brown County.

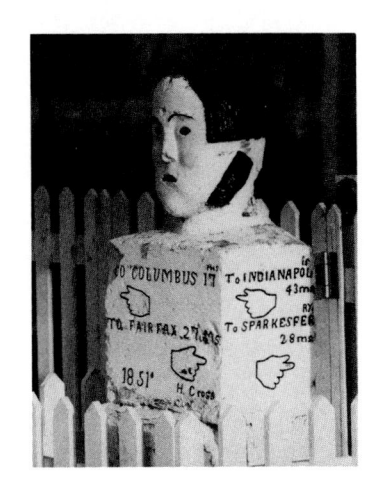

The Carl Brummett Chain Saw Repair Service Shop at Bean Blossom.

The stone head carved by Henry Cross in 1851
marks the town of Stone Head on SR 135 south.

It was more than thirty years later that the Indiana Department of Conservation restocked deer in the county, resulting in the population of today. And long after Rapp Pane had passed into history, the stone bore witness to his deed. Lichens and moss began to cover it, and not until the 1970s was the stone rediscovered by Park Naturalist Mike Ellis, who now is the state naturalist for all Indiana state parks at Indianapolis. The whereabouts of the stone is largely kept secret, for authorities fear it would be defaced if it were known to the public. So the stone deer of Brown County State Park remains a silent reminder of an era before the meaning of conservation was known. And it is a fitting tribute to the last deer in Brown County.

The Ghost Hand

In Ogle Hollow for three quarters of a century has roamed the ghost hand. Many people through the years, walking the woodland at night, have paused to listen to the sound of the hand crawling and scratching its way along the hillside.

Legend has it the hand and arm belonged to a farmer who once worked the land in Ogle Hollow and lost them during an accident. He lived, but the arm and hand were buried in a clay pot on the side of the hill. And the arm and hand have been, the story is told, searching for their owner ever since.

Deserter's Cave

At a remote location in Brown County State Park is Deserter's Cave or Copperhead Haven. The shallow sandstone cave which lies along a steep sloping ridge is well protected from the elements. The sun's rays strike it at such an angle that it stays warmer than many places in the park, thus making it an ideal habitat for copperhead snakes. Park Naturalist Jim Eagelman says it's one of the best places in the area to find the poisonous snakes.

During the Civil War, however, the cave was named because it became the hangout of two deserters from the Union army. Their names have been obscured by the years, but the story has lived down through the ages. And apparently, they lived out the war in the cave and afterward returned to normal lives.

Local historians had some doubt about the authenticity of the story, but a few years ago Jack Weddle, a high school teacher interested in such matters, did an intensive search of the cave and did find a metal button from a Union army uniform, which at least gives some credence to the story.

Fair Game

Two backwoods Brown Countians were hunting along Nebo Ridge one warm autumn day when they came upon a beautiful naked woman strolling through the woods.

Startled, she exclaimed: "What are you doing here?"

"Hunting for game, " they replied.

There was a brief silence.

"Well," she said, "I'm game!"

And so they shot her.

Peddler's Ghost Wagon

On a late October day around the turn of the century, a group of young people were standing on a bridge near Helmsburg watching the harvest moon, when they heard the rumbling of a wagon, drawn by trotting horses. It grew louder and louder, and the youngsters ran to the end of the bridge over Bean Blossom Creek to let it pass, for it sounded as though it were bearing down upon them. Just after they reached the end of the bridge, the wagon rumbled past and the sound soon died. But no wagon had passed; it was only the sound.

Since that time, the sound of the rumbling wagon has been heard many times by many different people. And it's always the same description. It's the ghost wagon of Brown County, and it belongs, so legend has it, to an old peddler who was murdered as he made his rounds one October day. And thus the wagon is more apt to be heard during October than at any other time, although there have been a few reports of it during other seasons. No one has ever seen a thing, but the sound is real and unmistakably a rumbling wagon; at least no one has questioned it to this date.

The road to Elkinsville in the southern part of the county offers a real country road atmosphere at any time of the year, even in winter.

If Brown County has a ghost house, the Sarah Jane Waltman house at Bean Blossom, well over a hundred years old, must be it. On Halloween, stories are told among local folks about goblins seen around the house, and witches sometimes appear there. It was on the porch of this house that Ben Kanter stood when he shot James Jenkins of the Dillinger gang with a 12-gauge shotgun.

The refurbished old Deckard home overlooking Lake Monroe is one of the stateliest houses in the county. Some claim it is haunted.

The Owl and the Postman

The story has been related to me of a legendary owl which breeds bad omen on Kelley Hill. The story has been passed down from generation to generation, but it seems there was an owl that used to sit just above the rutted roadway during the olden days of Brown County before there were hard-surfaced roads. And one day as the mail carrier was passing by, the owl swooped down and called to the mail carrier. And he called back. And no one ever saw him again. His team and mail wagon reached the post office at Belmont, but the mail carrier was missing.

The Watcher

One of the most persistent ghost stories in Brown County is that of The Watcher. A dozen different descriptions and stories have been circulated over the years about The Watcher, but all of them have placed the critter in Van Buren Township not far north of the Van Buren School.

Most tellers of the ghost story, or people who have had experiences with The Watcher, describe him as a man about eight to ten feet tall, wearing all black. Some say he wears a cape.

The Watcher, most people who have seen him or had experiences with him say, is a good ghost. Normally when he's seen, it's to warn of impending tragedy or disaster. For instance, one report is that he appeared to a family just shortly before their home burned, and because he frightened them, they were able to escape the flames, for they could not sleep that night.

Shoot-out at Bean Blossom

Probably the most exciting thing that ever happened at Bean Blossom during all of history was the big shoot-out in September of 1933, when the country was still in the midst of the Great Depression. When all was done, one man had been killed and another critically injured, with the townspeople armed behind locked doors and waiting for the next episode.

It all began when a massive jailbreak, engineered by Mooresville bank robber John Dillinger, was staged at the Michigan City state prison, springing some of the Dillinger gang. A great chase ensued with law officers in hot pursuit. At Indianapolis, some of the gang decided to spring a decoy. If they could push one of the gang out of the car, perhaps the law would stop to pick him up and thereby give Dillinger and his cronies a little more headway.

James Jenkins, whose father was a minister at Bedford, was elected and shoved from the car. But the chase did not stop; the law ignored Jenkins and kept right on after the Dillinger car.

Jenkins made his way to the south side of the city where he hitched a ride with an Indiana University student. Along the way, according to the story, Jenkins kicked the student out of the car and drove on by himself. The car ran out of gas, and since Jenkins had no money with him, he abandoned it and hitched a ride to near Bean Blossom.

The word had already reached town that the Dillinger gang was on the loose. And when someone spotted Jenkins near Bean Blossom, he was immediately suspect.

Jack McDonald, owner of the Bean Blossom IGA Store, remembers the stories he was told quite well. Although he was only a small chap at the time, he was in the McDonald's Grocery, located at the same place as the present IGA, with his mother when the incident occurred.

"My father [Herb McDonald] had just taken over the grocery a short time before," he said. "And when somebody ran into the store and said there was a suspicious-looking character on the street that might be one of the Dillinger gang, my dad and Ivan [Duck] Bond grabbed my dad's old 12-gauge shotgun and got in our car out front. When they got near the stranger, they stopped and before my dad could say how-do-you-do, the stranger said: 'Hold it right there, Mister,' and suddenly produced a .38 cal. snubnose revolver from inside his coat.

"My Dad ducked down in the car, and Duck Bond was doing his own ducking. But he wasn't quick enough and a shot caught my dad in the upper right shoulder. Jenkins might have killed him, but one of our neighbors—Ben Kanter—had come out on his porch and saw what was going on. And about that time, he brought out his gun and shot Jenkins right through the head.

"Meantime, my mother had stashed us kids down behind the counter and locked the door to the store . . . and the next thing we knew, my dad was beating on the door trying to get in. He was bleeding badly, and we rushed him over to Columbus to Doc Overshiner to get him patched up.

"By the time McDonald got back to town, Bean Blossom looked like an armed camp. Everybody in town had gotten out their guns. Men clustered about, all armed with guns, their womenfolk at home behind locked doors. Everybody was sure since Ben Kanter had killed Jenkins, a known member of the Dillinger gang, that the whole gang would be coming to wreak revenge. The showdown, everyone thought, was imminent. It was only a matter of hours. Everyone was sure of it. And they were going to be ready for them.

"When we got back home," Jack McDonald laughed, "there were even men lying under our front porch armed with shotguns. There were people on the roofs of the buildings. It was something to see. We didn't know there were so many people in Bean Blossom."

Fact is, there weren't that many people in Bean Blossom. People in Nashville and Helmsburg who wanted to get in on the excitement had come here. Even some of McDonald's friends in Indianapolis drove down, bringing their own arsenals with them, which didn't help matters any. Since the Bean Blossom people didn't know them, that in itself almost broke into open bloodshed.

"Strangers coming down from Indianapolis asking to see my dad were immediately suspect," said Jack McDonald. "And some of 'em nearly got shot just being inquisitive."

For several days, apprehension ran high at Bean Blossom. But the Dillinger gang had gone to Ohio and had their hands full with other matters. And since Jenkins was relatively unimportant to them, they never came that way, at least as far as anybody knew.

Meantime, Jenkins, who was not killed outright, was brought to Nashville and actually died there a few hours later. His father came up from Bedford and claimed the body. Later the preacher came to talk to Herb McDonald and told him how sorry he was that all the shooting came about. And that was the last time the McDonalds ever encountered the Dillinger gang. But it was a day still remembered in Bean Blossom, and probably will be for a long time to come.

It's somewhat ironic that, years later in 1975, the John Dillinger Museum was opened to the public in Nashville. It's been one of the major attractions ever since. And while Dillinger had no direct connection with Brown County, the shoot-out at Bean Blossom is one of the displays in the museum, complete with newspaper clippings, pictures, etc.

Jenkins' gun is not there; Herb McDonald had that for many years until his home was broken into a few years back and the gun stolen. Its whereabouts are still unknown. But Jack McDonald has the slug taken from his father's shoulder in the shoot-out.

The Roberts Legend

Legends are still being born in Brown County; one of the latest is the mysterious Roberts case which has a way of renewing itself from time to time. The mystery began in November 1970 when the body of a man many thought was that of Nashville businessman and former Brown County sheriff Clarence Roberts was found in the burned-out garage at the Roberts' home on Grandma Barnes Road. But Brown County coroner Earl Bond and deputy coroner Jack Bond, his son, differed on whether the body was actually Clarence Roberts. Consequently, the death certificate was never signed.

Then began a ten-year court battle by Mrs. Geneva Roberts, the wife of Clarence, to collect almost a million dollars of insurance money. The case was never settled, since she could never prove to authorities the body was that of her husband.

On November 29, 1980, a second mystery fire occurred, destroying the modest home of Geneva Roberts who had moved to another part of the county on SR 135 south. Two bodies were found in the rubble. They were identfied as Clarence and Geneva Roberts. And there was, according to police, strong evidence the second fire was arson, as was the first.

Although pathologists have identified the body of the man in the fire as that of Clarence Roberts, many local folks, including some of his own relatives, believe it was not. And if it was, who was the man found in the fire at the Roberts' home ten years earlier?

Police had had the Roberts' home under surveillance for the past six years on SR 135 south—the one that burned in 1980—and had reported seeing a man closely resembling Roberts coming and going at the home during all that time. But they had never been able to determine positive identity since the house was guarded by a vicious guard dog.

Many who knew Roberts and his wife well said once away he would never have returned since the two of them were never able to get along without constant bickering and fighting.

So some major questions remain unanswered and authorities admit many of those questions may never be answered. Helen Ayers, a reporter for the *Brown County Democrat* covering the matter, listed the questions arising from the case in a published story:

—Who was the man found in the 1970 fire and how was he killed?
—Who killed him?
—Were Geneva and Clarence Roberts killed by someone else who then burned the house to hide the evidence in November of 1980?

—Geneva Roberts' home was guarded by a reportedly vicious dog. Prior to the fire (which occurred shortly before midnight) did the dog sense nothing unusual about what was going on in the house? If it had, would it have barked and alerted relatives who lived nearby?
—Did Clarence and Geneva Roberts have a reconciliation and then commit suicide together?
—Who is the mystery man who had been seen at her residence for the past six years or so?
—Did Geneva have a lover who killed both Clarence and Geneva when he found them together?
—Or is it possible Clarence's brother, Carson, with whom he was quite close, is correct, and this was not Clarence Roberts' body found in the fire at all? Is he instead, as was reported by some witnesses over the past ten years, now living in the mountains of Mexico, or at some other place?

The mystery probably will never be entirely resolved. In the meantime, it has all the rich ingredients for the creation of yet another Brown County legend that likely will deepen and become even more embellished with time.

Superstitions

It's a sin to burn sassafras wood. If you do, the devil will sit astraddle the roof of your house.

When the katydids begin to holler, frost will follow in six weeks.

A live chicken snake put in a barrel of cider will keep it from spoilin' and keep it sweet; also provides the snake with a frolickin' good time.

A whistlin' woman and a crowin' hen
Are sure to come to some bad end

If you get a persistent nose itch, it means company is coming soon.

If a rooster crows before going to bed, it means he'll awaken with a wet head.

It's bad luck to leave a friend's house by a separate door than you entered.

A dirty sock worn around the neck when retiring to bed will cure a sore throat; also open up the nose and maybe turn the stomach.

Never use a tree for firewood that has been struck by lightning. It belongs to the devil.

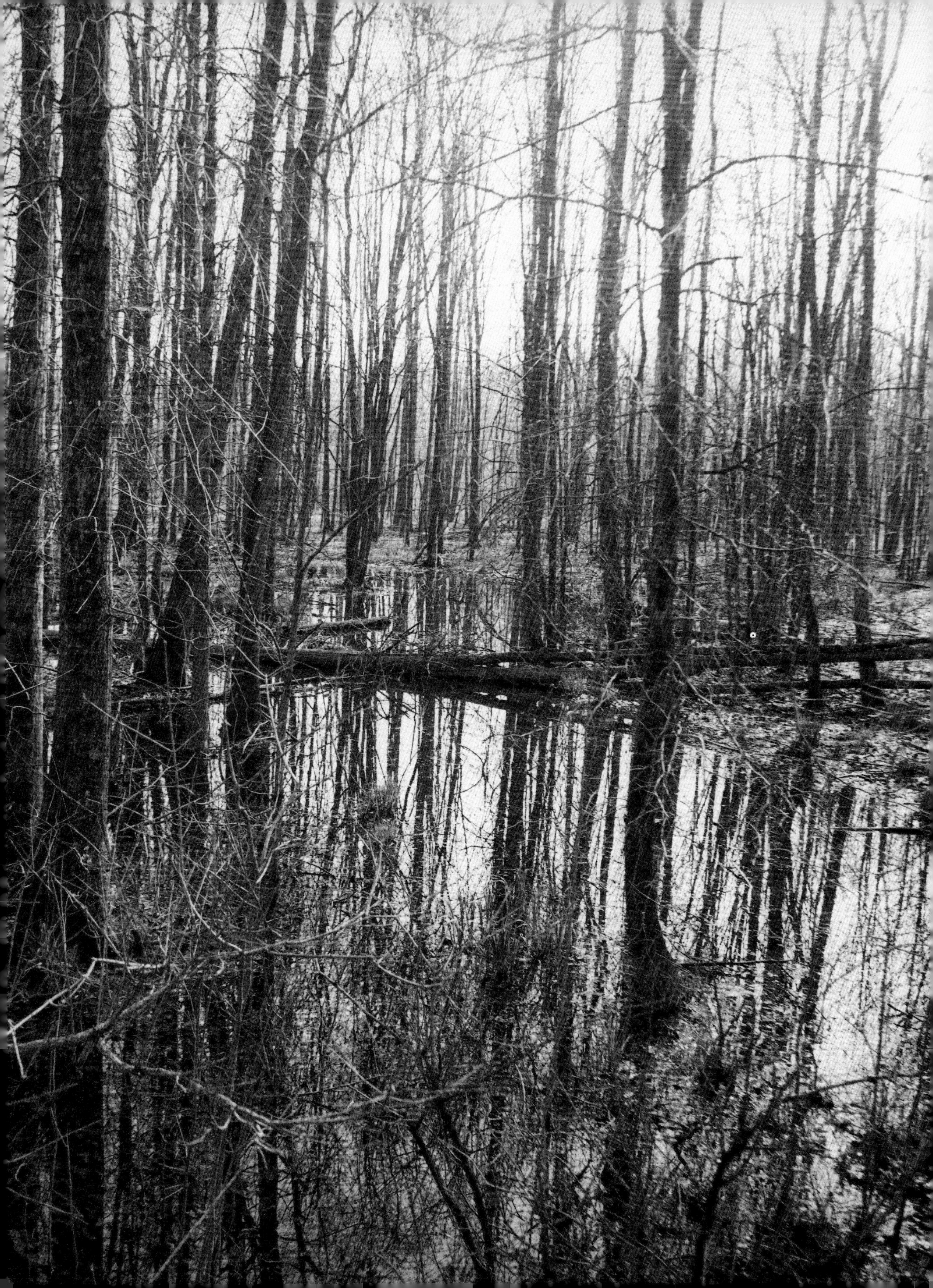

Potpourri

Brown is a Healthy Place

7 It's a fact, according to the 1979 edition of the *Indiana Fact Book,* that Brown County has the cleanest air in the state, perhaps even in the entire Midwest.

In a breakdown of major point source emissions into the air, including particulate matter, sulfur dioxide, nitrogen oxides, hydrocarbons, and carbon monoxide, Brown County is the only county in Indiana which lists zero in all categories.

So when you get to Brown County, folks, breathe deeply. It's probably the highest quality and cleanest air you'll ever experience.

Demise of the Rattlesnake

The eastern timber rattlesnake has been as much a part of Brown County as any other resident for hundreds of years, but Mr. Rattlesnake has virtually disappeared.

Mike Ellis, Indiana State naturalist who formerly was the Brown County State Park naturalist, says much of the prime habitat in the park was destroyed a few years ago when new camping sites were built and the area was bulldozed.

"A lot of snakes of various kinds were killed then," recalled Mike. "It was a prime habitat for the timber rattler and the copperhead, as well as for some non-poisonous snakes. In fact, I firmly believe it was among the last habitats for the timber rattler in Brown County."

With so much habitat being destroyed and so much pressure from people to kill off the rattler, it may become a threatened species of wildlife in Indiana. "All many people think of doing once they see a snake, particularly a rattler, is kill it," said Ellis. "And the rattler is as important as any other form of life. There's no reason why they should be wiped out."

Brown's Butterfly Tree

At the Matterhorn, one of Brown County's remote high places, is the butterfly tree, a mighty white oak on which thousands of migrating monarchs gather each autumn as they fly to their wintering grounds in Mexico. Mary Ann Matter, owner and resident of the Matterhorn, considers it one of the highlights of the year at her Brown County home.

"It is simply one of the greatest things you'll ever see," she told me a few years ago. "They come all at once, gathering across the meadow from the north at dusk. They cluster on the one tree mainly, but sometimes a few gather on nearby trees. They choose the south and west branches of the tree and cluster mainly on one limb. Sometimes I think it will break, there are so many of them—thousands, thousands!"

Until a few years ago little was known of the monarchs, but a Canadian professor, Dr. Fred Urquhart of Toronto, has carried out extensive studies which show that most of the monarchs gather in Mexico just north of Mexico City, along the California coast between Monterey and Los Angeles, and that others make an unbelievable flight across the Gulf of Mexico from the Florida Keys to the Yucatan Peninsula to spend the winter. En route, they have certain locations where they like to rest, and that does not change from year to year, even though the same butterfly does not live for more than one annual migration.

"They will come," Ms. Matter says, "to the very same tree year after year." She first began noticing them about 1966, but she doesn't know how many years they'd been coming there before that. They usually come, she said, about the middle of September, arriving at dusk, and by sunrise the following morning, most are gone, flying away to the south. The Matterhorn is located just off Greasy Creek Road.

The wetlands south of Story.

The Copper Worm

An old-timer was out scouring the hills in southern Brown County one spring day and ran across one of his neighbors, who inquired what he was doing.

"I'm out looking for copper worms," the old-timer answered.

"Copper worms?"

"Yep, I'm needin' a spring tonic . . . and I ain't had no luck findin' any copper worms all year."

The fact is, the copper worms have all but disappeared in Brown County, but at one time there may have been at least a dozen or two operating on any given day. The copper worm, of course, was the illegal moonshine whiskey still.

A seventy-nine-year-old man living in Bloomington related how he used to make stills for folks in Brown County. A metalsmith, he told me in 1980 he'd made more than 30 stills when he was a young man for folks in Brown County. "It wasn't no big business," he said. "Fact is, I think most of 'em was for family use. But there was 'shine in them hills when I was young."

Sheriff Rex Kritzer, who grew up in Brown County, remembers running across barrels of fermenting mash, when he was just a boy out hunting. But the last moonshine still raided by authorities, he believes, was 15 to 20 years ago near Peoga in the northeastern section of the county. And that one was being operated in a garage, he said.

Since many of the folks who settled early in Brown County had come directly from Kentucky, Tennessee, and the mountains of the Carolinas, it was natural that moonshine whiskey be made here. For it was a way of life there. Many of the people of Appalachia considered it their constitutional right to make corn squeezin's, and they carried the art with them wherever they went. So Brown County has had its share of copper worms. But copper worms now are an endangered species, indeed.

Land of Christmas Trees

In the 1950s and '60s, Brown County became the proverbial land of Christmas trees. Land was cheap, and a lot of people throughout the lower Midwest decided suddenly they could get rich growing Christmas trees. Among them was forester Don Goodwin, proprietor of Goodwin Tree Farm on SR 135 south.

At the height of the Christmas tree fad, more than 50 growers were located throughout the county, and hundreds, indeed, thousands of acres, mostly ridgetops, were planted in Scotch and white pine. The Hills O'Brown were turning a year-round green. Many of the remnants of those Christmas tree plantations still exist, but the trees were never harvested.

Don Goodwin describes it like any other get-rich-quick scheme. A lot of the people who decided to grow Christmas trees didn't know the first thing about it. All they thought you had to do was set the trees out, wait eight or ten years, and then harvest your fortune. "It doesn't quite work that way," he said.

Goodwin, the largest grower in the county today, harvests about 60,000 trees each year. And he plants about 35,000. Although no accurate figures are available, it's estimated about 80,000 Christmas trees are harvested in Brown County each year, most of them going to other points in Indiana as well as Kentucky, Tennessee, Alabama, and Florida. Some also go to Illinois.

"It's a year-round job," said Goodwin. "We're working the trees 12 months a year—pruning, trimming, spraying with artificial colors. And then the cutting begins about the first of November. By Thanksgiving, all the trees have been cut and the truckers have loaded them for shipping."

Joe Vasquez, a Mexican who first came to the county and worked for Goodwin, has now become a landowner and grower himself. And he probably is the second largest grower in Brown.

Most of the trees grown in Brown County are either Scotch or white pine. "They unquestionably make the best Christmas trees," said Goodwin. "Especially the white pine. But that's partially personal preference, I guess," he said.

Brown's Public Voice

As far as is known, Brown County never had a town crier, but there are those who claim residents shed their share of tears over the newspapers. There have been a pack of them over the years, all dedicated to keeping the hill and hollow folks posted on the latest happenings.

The first newspaper was *The Spy*, founded about 1854 by S. A. Amour. Following its demise came others with such names as *The Hickory Withe, Evangelical Republican, Nashville Union, Nashville Star, Nashville Democrat, Jacksonian, Jacksonian Democrat,* the *Brown County Republican,* and the *Brown County Banner*. And of course, those were followed by the county's present contribution to the Fourth Estate, the *Brown County Democrat*.

Excerpts from the Brown County Sheriff's Log

One of the most popular and entertaining items in Brown County's weekly newspaper, *The Democrat,* is the Sheriff's Log. For those unfamiliar with such matters, the log is merely a chronological listing of events as they transpire each day in the sheriff's office. While many are simply routine, there are always some gems among each week's listings, and a few have been selected at random for inclusion here.

Lady from England came in to take a picture of the sheriff. Said they have no sheriff there.

Man reported a demented and suicidal deer tried to kill itself by running into the side of his truck. (How is your truck? It's OK, I think, I can't see any damage.) Said he almost got several other deer also. Unable to advise if the deer was killed, since there was too much traffic to stop. Told the man that whenever he wanted to get to Bloomington in the future he should consider going to Brownstown to Bedford to Bloomington. (One can't be too careful with regards to the kind of deer we have around here.)

Man reported he saw some Iranians.

Visitor from Michigan advises black-and-white dog on corner of Van Buren and Main looks extremely tired and distressed and has swollen paws. (Owner is advised to go and get her tired dog.)

Active burglar alarm on Lanam Ridge Rd., but two big dogs are guarding the house and won't let deputy out of car.

Woman said someone was in her car on Woodland Lake Road who, she believes, is stripping her car. Deputy said there was a goat in the car when he arrived.

(12:35 A.M.) Man called and said he just put on a pot of coffee if any of the officers are in the area and want coffee.

Man reported to be riding a horse in the recreation hall in the state park. He is disturbing the square dance.

(11/4/80)—Election Day) Someone called in on fire phone wanting to know "Do they have anything to eat at the voting polls at Gatesville?"

(2:54 P.M.) A raccoon has fallen into a grease barrel at a local restaurant and is in bad shape.

Woman said dogs were chasing the llamas on Old Helmsburg Rd.

Trouble reported at the city dump. Someone abandoned a person there.

Woman called from Illinois and wanted to know if it is storming in Nashville.

People at the south gate of the park report a horse fell over the hill, and nobody has been able to find the rider.

(12:57 A.M.) Man phones that he hears screaming near his home.

(1:12 A.M.) Deputy has located two males and one female who state they were singing, not screaming.

Lady wants to know if it is illegal for a cycle rider to wear a spiked bracelet. Deputy says to tell her that golfers wear spiked shoes.

Woman said there is a dead cow on Rt. 135 North that has been there for 3 or 4 days and would like to have something done about it because it does not look very good.

Ramada Inn reported a person just kicked in a door and broke a window and then took off on foot across the parking lot. Person was mad because he couldn't get a sandwich.

Woman reports she found a dead dog in her bed.

(1:30 P.M.) Woman at bank reported receiving a telephone call on an unpublished number advising them there is going to be a bank robbery at 3 P.M. Said she at first thought this was a prank call from the branch bank, but it wasn't.

Antiques are one of the major attractions of Brown County.

The outbuildings still retain the old-timey appearance. This one is located at Stone Head.

Commander Rice called about his work schedule. (Who is Commander Rice?)

Girl at restaurant requests a conservation officer. An owl is sitting on the pizza oven.

(7:45 P.M.) Man reported gunshots coming from inside a residence in Helmsburg.

(7:57 P.M.) Deputy said man said he did shoot gun with a piece of toilet paper in it but will not do it again.

A deer is reported in the Underwood Stables, and they want a "strong" conservation officer to remove it.

(8:31 P.M.) Man observed two male subjects carrying a television wrapped in a blanket out of woods. Subjects told the man the television was a gift for their mother.

Man wants deputy (any deputy) to meet him so that he can borrow $5 or $10.

Man wants to know if sheriff would like to come watch his snakes eat.

(9:27 P.M.) Man requests Nashville town marshal go to restaurant and check the stove to see if he left a pot of beans on the stove.

(9:55 P.M.) Deputy advises he entered the restaurant and turned off the beans. Restaurant operator advised of this and says deputy gets a free meal.

Coroner wanted to talk to an "old time game warden" about a squirrel that doesn't have any hair.

Man wanted the sheriff to "stay put." Said he wanted to bring in his baby to show it off.

Woman reported a man came in her house and pulled out a knife. Said she knocked the knife out of his hand and grabbed a gun, then the man grabbed the knife and took off. Also said to tell the sheriff he can come and get a goose.

(8:38 P.M.) Sweetwater Lake woman has lost her dog, and he has never been out at night by himself.

Bartholomew County woman said she had had a telephone call from their sheriff's office that her car had been abandoned in Brown County. She said she did not even own a car, so it could not be hers.

Woman said she had just found a dead horse in her pond.

(11:45 P.M.) Someone was reported sleeping in the courthouse.

(12:37 A.M.) Advised sleeper (above) to go to the courthouse restrooms instead of walking the streets so that he can keep warm.

(12:49 A.M.) Same man came in station and wanted to be arrested.

(1:54 A.M.) Deputy took the man to his own home so that he will not have to walk the streets of Nashville tonight.

Man called about another man at the state park, on the ground, saying he is thirsty. Conservation officer talked to man on ground and he said he was all right and had just been released from jail. Deputy does not want him back.

(7:30 P.M.) Man reported a raccoon that keeps coming up on his porch and eating his cat's food and fighting with his cat. Would like for a conservation officer to come to Greasy Creek and live trap the coon.

(7:40 P.M.) Same man called back and said to disregard the trap. Said his cat watches the raccoon eat and that it is kind of pretty to see.

Vintage Drug Store

Visitors and customers at the Nashville Hook's Drug Store may, by just strolling to the rear of the store, enter a different era, an old-time vintage pharmacy little different from John A. Hook's first drug store established in Indianapolis in 1900. Open seven days a week, it is a living restoration of that first store. Today, the system includes 250 pharmacies in more than 110 Indiana communities and in neighboring Illinois. The Nashville old-time drug store contains an old-fashioned soda fountain, antiquish candy jars, medicine bottles, and a décor right from yesteryear. A copy of a painting done by Brown County artist C. Carey Cloud, depicting Hook's first drug store, hangs in the Nashville store.

Country Store

While the country store with the potbellied stove has virtually disappeared in Brown County as well as in other places, the one place most resembling that atmosphere is Henderson's Bait Shop on SR 46 in Schooner Valley. In cold weather, Bill and his son, James, keep the woodburning stove red hot, and there's always a small group of storytellers about—or sometimes checkers players—to while away the time during the winter months. While the shop certainly doesn't fill the bill as a general store, it does offer a variety of bait, tackle, and hunting paraphernalia.

McDonald's Grocery

McDonald's Grocery at Bean Blossom is the oldest continuous store in Brown County, and from the outset in 1891, it has been operated by the McDonald family. Current owner is Jack McDonald, whose grandfather, Cass McDonald, founded the store. His great-grandfather also worked in it. Jack's daughter, Diana Lynn, currently works in the store, making it five generations of McDonalds associated with the business.

Jack's father, Herb, operated a huckster business out of the store, first with mule team and wagon and then later with an old Chevrolet truck, covering just about every section of Brown County. With the huckster wagon, he carried a bugle from which he'd blow a few notes now and then to let his customers know he was headed their way.

The first McDonald's Grocery building still stands at Bean Blossom; it's the old red building on the corner of the parking lot where is located the McDonald's IGA; it now houses a gift shop. The new store was built in 1962.

Simple Cures

For colds or a sore throat, peel the bark from a slippery elm branch and chew it vigorously. Children in Brown County used to use the expended gum balls to throw at teachers, or other children in school.

For headache, chew willow twigs until your ears ring. Willow, incidentally, contains salicylic acid, one of the ingredients of aspirin.

To alleviate arthritis, old-timers recommend you drink a mixture of honey, vinegar, and moonshine whiskey every morning before breakfast.

For chest congestion, heat mutton tallow and apply it directly to the chest. A mixture of mutton tallow, soot, pine tar, camphor, turpentine, and lard applied as a poultice on the chest also will break up chest congestion as well as anything else you might have. It'll also fumigate your house and rid it of rats, mice, wasps, bedbugs, and roaches.

A vinegar cocktail taken daily cures many ills and prevents many others, including arthritis, nervousness, kidney or bladder stones, varicose veins or hardening of the arteries, buildup of cholesterol, heart disease, loss of hair, and it maintains virility. Mix 2 teaspoons of natural apple cider vinegar and one teaspoon of unprocessed honey in a 6-ounce glass of water.

For hiccups, eat a teaspoon of peanut butter.

To treat poison ivy or poison oak, take six or eight leaves of nightshade weed and cook with butter for five minutes. Then add four ounces of milk. Let remain on stove for about 10 minutes. When cool, apply to rash. Repeat twice a day.

If you perchance should pick up body lice, there's an easy way to rid your clothing of them. Find a large anthill, take a stick and stir it up, and then put all your clothing on the anthill, including your shoes. Go sleep in the shade or douse yourself in a cold pond for two to three hours. Ants will kill the lice and eat the eggs.

To remove warts, dip them in stump water twice a day—at sunrise and sunset.

For nosebleed, dry and crumble the leaves of hazel bush and stuff up your nose.

For bleeding, take a dried puffball mushroom and put on the wound; seal with gum from a wild cherry tree.

Food & Recipes

8 In an area that remained pioneer in spirit for a much longer time than other parts of the nation, it was natural that the people living in Brown County relied upon the foods available to them in the woodlands and fields. Nuts, wild game, and various types of wild plants, including wild carrot, asparagus, dandelion, pokeweed, wild kale, blackberries, huckleberries, wild raspberries, and many other types of natural food were readily obtainable in season.

A great deal of simple creativity went on in the kitchen, too, as housewives attempted to find new ways to make simple foods more appealing and give the family a variety of dishes. I've looked diligently in many places for some of those early down-to-earth recipes that are typically Brown County, and I'm presenting them for your cooking pleasures here. While some were certainly used in other places, they are typically Brown County recipes. I haven't tried each of them, however, so I cannot vouch for their taste, or your efforts.

The recipes were collected at random from many places, but several of them were provided by Mrs. Mary Richhart of Spearsville; the mushroom recipes were donated by Brown County's expert on mycology, Judge Sam Rosen.

Acorn Meal

Acorns can be divided into two broad classifications: White Oaks and Red Oaks. The chief difference is that White Oak acorns mature in one year and are much sweeter than the Red Oak acorns, which mature in two years. No matter, the processing is the same for both. The acorns first have to be peeled. This can be done with a sturdy knife or a nut cracker and nut pick. Wash them once after they are peeled to eliminate all loose skins and bits of shells, then grind them. After the acorns have been passed through the grinder once, they are ready to be processed to remove the bitter taste. This bitter taste, as many people know, is caused by tannin. Tannin, however, will dissolve in water. The next step then is to boil them. Dump the ground acorn into a kettle of water and boil until the water turns dark brown. Change the water then and repeat the boiling procedure. Change again when the water is grossly discolored. Keep this up until the acorn meal is sweet or neutral to the taste. Usually three changes of water with two minutes of boiling between changes will eliminate the bitterness. When the bitterness is gone, the meal is ground fine, and the resulting flour can be made into bread, flapjacks, or cake. Processed coarse ground acorns can be used as a substitute for nuts in cooking, as boiled breakfast food, and in many other ways.

Baked Apple Butter

Combine 16 cups of applesauce, preferably homemade; 2 tablespoons lemon juice; ½ cup apple cider; 8 cups sugar; 2 tablespoons cinnamon; 1 tablespoon cloves; 1 tablespoon allspice; and 1 teaspoon nutmeg. Heat, stirring constantly, until mixture comes to boil. Place in an enameled pan and bake in a moderate oven (350°) for about two hours, or until no liquid separates from a spoonful dropped on a saucer. Seal in hot, sterilized jars. Makes about 6 pints.

Baked Beans

Wash 1 pound of beans and soak over night. Cook slowly for one hour, then place in an earthen bean pot, season with 1½ cupfuls brown sugar, 1 tablespoonful salt, 1 small teaspoonful cinnamon, 1 small onion cut into bits, 1 pint canned tomatoes, and lay a generous piece of smoked ham or strips of bacon on top. Bake in a moderate oven for several hours, keeping plenty of liquid by adding water if necessary.

Fried Biscuits

Dissolve 3 packages of dry yeast in ½ cup lukewarm water. Then add ½ cup lard or shortening, 1 quart milk, ½ cup sugar, 6 teaspoons salt, and 7-9 cups of flour. Cover and let rise in warm place until about double. Work into biscuits and drop into hot fat until browned. Temperature of fat should be only slightly higher than 350°; if too hot, biscuits will be soggy in center. This recipe makes about seven dozen. Biscuits may be frozen individually and stored in plastic bags.

Blackberry Dumplings

Pour 1 quart of blackberries in a deep pan, add enough sugar to sweeten and a lump of butter half the size of an egg. Boil two minutes. Make a rich biscuit dough, roll and cut into squares. Add the berry filling, make into dumplings, and boil until done. Serve hot.

Blackberry Pudding

Beat 3 eggs light and stir into 2 cupfuls milk. Sift 1 quart flour with 5 teaspoonfuls baking powder and beat this gradually into eggs and milk. Dredge 3 cupfuls blackberries with flour and stir into batter. Turn into greased pudding dish. Bake covered for 1 hour, uncover and brown. Eat with hard sauce made by working together 2 tablespoonfuls butter and 1 cupful sugar to a white cream. Beat in the juice of 1 lemon and a pinch of nutmeg. Set in cool place until needed.

Blackbird Pie

Dress and clean well a dozen blackbirds as you would pigeons; split each in half, put them into stew pan with plenty of water and bring to a boiling point; skim off rising scum, then add salt and pepper to season, some minced parsley, a chopped onion, and about three whole cloves; add about 1 cup diced salt pork and boil until tender; thicken broth with browned flour and boil; add 2 tablespoons butter, mix and remove from fire; cool; add 2 cups diced potatoes. Grease baking dish and put in alternate layers of boned birds and potatoes, moistening well each layer with some of the rich broth; cover with rich pastry crust, with slits or openings in the top, and bake in oven until cooked and browned. Or baking dish may be both lined and covered with pastry.

Buttermilk Cake

Mix together 2½ cups of sifted flour, 1½ cups of sugar, ½ cup of cocoa, 1½ teaspoonfuls of soda, and 1 teaspoon of salt; sift 4 times; then add 1½ cups of buttermilk, ½ cup of melted lard; beat well and add vanilla to suit your taste. Bake in a moderate oven.

Catfish Soup

Cut up two or three pounds of catfish; add two quarts cold water, one sliced onion, one chopped celery stalk, salt and pepper, herbs (bay leaf, parsley, thyme), one cup milk, two tablespoons butter or fat. Place all ingredients into stew pan and put on slow fire. Stir occasionally and cook until fish is ready to serve. Serve hot.

Baked Coon

Boil coon in water with one onion, and salt, until tender. Remove and place in shallow pan, sprinkle with a little sage, add one cup hot water. Precook about six medium-size sweet potatoes, cut in half, and place around coon. Bake in hot oven for 20 minutes.

Green Corn

In cooking corn on the ear, leave on the last layer of husks, turn back and remove the silk. Then replace husks and tie with a string over end of corn. Boil until tender and serve at once. You will find this makes delicious corn. The husks give a flavor that is not present when corn is cooked without the husks. Some cooks husk the corn in the usual way and then throw in a few husks to boil with the corn.

Corn Pudding

To 1 can corn add 2 beaten eggs, 1 teaspoonful salt, a few dashes of pepper, 1½ tablespoonfuls butter, 1 pint hot milk. Turn into a buttered baking dish and bake in a slow oven until the pudding is firm.

Rich Chocolate Fudge

Melt ¼ cake chocolate in a pan, and add ¼ cup butter, ½ cup rich milk, and 3 cups brown sugar in order named and boil. When it will form a soft ball when tested in cold water, remove from fire. Let cool a little and beat until thick. Pour into a buttered shallow pan, cut into small squares, and let cool.

Bird's Nest Pudding

Butter a pudding dish and half fill it with apples pared and diced. Make a batter of 1 pint flour sifted and mixed with 2 teaspoonfuls baking powder, 1 tablespoonful sugar, ½ teaspoonful salt, ½ pint of sweet milk, 3 tablespoonfuls melted butter, and 1 well-beaten egg. Pour this over the apples, bake one hour and serve with cream or milk and sugar. This is very fine.

Maple Fudge

Follow recipe for Rich Chocolate Fudge (above) except leave out chocolate; substitute 1 cup maple syrup for 1 cup of the brown sugar; or use 2½ cups brown sugar and ½ cup shaved maple sugar.

Hamburger and Mushroom Flambé

Joan Rosen offers this recipe for hamburger or steak and mushroom flambé. Ingredients include 1 teaspoon butter, ½ cup raw mushrooms (boletta, puffball, etc.), 1 ounce warm brandy, hamburger or steak. Sprinkle a heated, heavy fry pan with salt. Pan broil lean small steak or hamburger until almost done, turning only once. Add butter and raw mushrooms. Place these to one side of the pan and sauté briefly. Pour the warm brandy over this and flame. Serve the meat topped with the mushrooms and pan drippings.

Hickory Nut Cake

Cream ¼ cup shortening, ½ cup butter, and 2 cups sugar together. Sift 2½ cups sifted cake flour, 2½ teaspoons baking powder, and ¾ teaspoon salt together three times. Combine 1 cup milk and 1 teaspoon vanilla. Add flour mixture to creamed mixture, alternating with the milk and vanilla. (Alternating should be done in thirds, starting and finishing with the dry ingredients.) Add 1 cup finely chopped hickory nuts to the last portion of the dry ingredients just before adding. Beat only until all ingredients are well blended. Beat 5 egg whites until stiff but not dry. Stir approximately 1 cup of the beaten whites into the batter to lighten it, then gently fold in the rest.

Turn batter into two greased and floured 9" round cake pans and spread batter evenly. Bake at 350° for ½ hour, or until cake pulls away from the sides of the pans. Cool on rack for 5 minutes, then turn out of pans and cool completely. If desired, frost with Maple Frosting. Garnish the top with additional chopped nuts.

Maple Frosting

Cream 6 tablespoons soft butter and 3 cups sifted confectioners' sugar together until smooth. Gradually add 6 tablespoons maple syrup and beat until consistency is right for spreading.

Hickory Nut Candy

Boil together 2 cupfuls sugar and ½ cupful water without stirring. When syrup will spin a thread, place pan in cold water, add lemon or vanilla extract and beat until white. Stir in 1 cupful nut meats, turn out on buttered plate and when cold cut into squares.

Maple Syrup Cake

Cream ½ cup butter, and gradually cream in ½ cup sugar. Without separating, beat 2 eggs, and add to the sugar-butter mixture; stir in 1 cup maple syrup. Heat ½ cup milk; sift and measure 2½ cups flour (about), add 2 teaspoons baking powder and ⅔ teaspoon soda, and sift again. Add flour and hot milk alternately, a little at a time, and completely mix. Bake in a round center-tube pan, and cover with Maple Icing.

Mayapples

Juice for jelly and drinking can be obtained by simmering, for 45 minutes, mayapples that have been washed and sliced. Stir the mixture occasionally, as it tends to stick. Pour the cooked mixture into a jelly bag and let drip into a pan overnight. The pulp that is left in the bag can be dumped out and pushed through a colander. This will separate the seeds and peels from the pulp. Make mayapple sauce from the pulp by adding cinnamon and sugar to taste. Jelly from the juice is made the same as any berry jelly.

Mush and Milk

Heat 1 quart of water to boiling point, add ½ teaspoonful salt, then stir in sifted corn meal, adding slowly to prevent lumps, stirring rapidly. Cook slowly for an hour or more. Serve in milk with any cooked dried fruits, such as prunes, raisins, or dried apricots.

Marinated Mushrooms

Ingredients include 1 pound mushrooms (these can be any local wild mushrooms, such as chanterettes, bolettas, puffballs, or even morels); 1 lemon; ¼ cup olive oil; 1 cup red or white wine vinegar; 2 cloves garlic, peeled; ½ tablespoon oregano; 5 black peppercorns; ½ tablespoon kosher salt; chopped parsley. Trim the stems and clean the mushrooms; cut a tic-tac-toe pattern into the caps. Add the mushrooms to a big pot with half the lemon, sliced into thin rounds; oil; wine vinegar; garlic; oregano; peppercorns; and salt. Heat over high heat until the mushrooms become dark. Turn off heat and let set. Cool to room temperature. Remove and discard the garlic, lemon slices, and peppercorns. The mushrooms can be made the day before and refrigerated until an hour before serving. Bring back to room temperature and garnish with the remaining lemon, cut in rounds or wedges, and fresh parsley. Serves 6.

Persimmon Pudding

Take 3 pints of persimmon pulp that has been run through the colander, add 2 cupfuls sugar, ½ cupful melted butter, 4 eggs, 1 cupful sour milk with 1 teaspoonful soda dissolved in it, and 2½ cupfuls flour. Bake in a moderate oven. Prepare a syrup made of 2 cupfuls sugar, 1 cupful water, 1 tablespoonful butter and boil until a thick syrup. Pour over pudding, replace in oven and let syrup cook into the pudding for a few minutes. This is very fine.

Roast Pigeons

Clean, leave the feet on, dip them in scalding water, strip off the skin, cross them, and tie them together below the breast bone, or cut them off. The head may remain on—if so, dip it in scalding water, and pick it clean; twist the wings back, put the liver between the right wing and the body, and turn the head under the other. Rub butter over each bird, salt and pepper. Split them, and put some water in the dripping pan—for each bird put in a large teaspoon of butter. Put before a hot fire, and let them roast quickly. Baste frequently; half an hour will do. When nearly done, baste with wheat flour and butter, so they may be nicely and easily browned.

Trail Potatoes (Broiled)

Cut cold boiled potatoes in slices lengthwise, one-fourth of an inch thick; dip each slice in flour; and lay them on a gridiron over a bright bed of coals; when both sides are browned, take them up on a hot dish; add a little bacon grease or butter, salt and pepper. Serve hot.

Sassafras Tea

Eight or ten roots, dropped into two or three quart kettle, covered with as much water as is desired, depending on the number you wish to serve. Let boil until tea is dark in color. These roots may be boiled over and over for days, as the flavor will last. Quarter roots over ½ inch diameter.

Snicker Doodles

Mix 2 cups white flour, 2 teaspoons baking powder, 1 cup brown sugar, 1 egg, ½ cup milk, 1 cup raisins, ½ cup butter, and hickory nut meats. Stir well, then place in oven and bake.

Vinegar Pie

Mix together 1 cupful granulated sugar, 3 or 4 tablespoonfuls vinegar, 2 teaspoonfuls lemon extract, 2 level tablespoonfuls cornstarch and slowly add 2 cupfuls boiling water, stirring constantly on the stove until the mixture gets thick. When cold, stir in yolks of 2 eggs and pour into 2 pie tins lined with good pastry. When baked, cool and cover with the beaten whites of eggs and sugar. Brown in a quick oven.

Kitchen Hints

Don't be afraid to try again if you fail again and again; success is the result of perseverance and application.

A little boiling water added to an omelette as it thickens will prevent its being tough.

Open canned fruit an hour or two before it is needed for use. It is far richer when the oxygen is thus restored to it.

Almonds are blanched by scalding them with boiling water.

To keep cookies from burning on the bottom, turn the baking pan upside down and bake on the bottom of the pan, and you will never do it any other way.

Put a handful or two of tissue paper, torn into shreds, in the bottom of the cookie jar. This allows the air to pass through, keeping the cookies crisp and good.

If the top of a cake is sprinkled with flour as it is turned from the pan, the icing will spread more easily and will not be so likely to run. Before the cake is iced, most of the flour should be wiped off.

Ginger cookies mixed with cold coffee instead of milk have a delicious taste.

In order to have potatoes always white, the kettle in which they are cooked should never be used for any other purpose.

A currycomb makes an excellent fish scraper.

Hot milk added to potatoes when mashing them will keep them from being soggy or heavy.

When making a steamed or boiled pudding, put a pleat in the cloth at the top to allow for the pudding to swell.

A pinch of soda stirred into milk that is to be boiled will keep it from curdling.

Heavy cakes are often the result of using damp fruit. After washing, currants and raisins should be left in a colander in a slightly warm place for twenty-four hours.

Before baking potatoes, peel them and rub with butter or bacon. The outside, when baked, will be a delicate brown, which can be eaten with the rest of the potato.

If the roasted potatoes are burst with a fork, they will be found much lighter and more digestible than if cut with a knife.

Pumpkins should be kept in a dry part of the cellar, apples in a moderately dry part; turnips should be kept in a damp part of the cellar.

To cut hard-boiled eggs in smooth slices, dip the knife in water.

An oven door should never be slammed when anything is baking.

When cooking lima beans, rice, etc., it is very provoking when they foam and splutter onto a clean stove. Drop into the kettle a small lump of butter, and there will be no boiling over.

Do not use newspapers to wrap about anything eatable.

By stewing some rhubarb in aluminumware pans and kettles, they may be cleaned and brightened; there yet remains to be manufactured a polish that will do the work better.

To keep icing soft, add a pinch of baking soda to the whites of the eggs before beating them, then beat and proceed in the usual way.

To keep a cake fresh for several weeks take it from the oven and, while still hot, pack it completely in brown sugar.

If soup is too salty, add slices of raw potatoes and boil a few minutes until saltiness is reduced to taste. The potatoes may then be used in many ways.

Save all liquids from mustard or spiced pickles and use them in salad dressings or for mixing with meat for sandwiches.

Save the liquor from pickled peaches, etc.; it may be used in places where wine was formerly used, such as mince pies, sauces, etc.

In cooking vegetables, cover those that grow under the ground, as turnips, onions, etc.; leave uncovered those that grow above the ground.

When cream will not whip, add the white of an egg, both being chilled to same temperature; it will then whip quite readily.

Finding morels is one of the delights of spring.
(*Bill Scifres*)

Sassafras trees stand as stark sentinels awaiting spring along Freeman Ridge Road. Tea is made from the roots of the tree.